BILLY GRAHAM has probably preach any person in the history of Christianity. Certainly the extraordinary success of his Crusades for Christ marks him as one of the most influential religious figures of the century.

Millions have heard his stirring message on radio and TV and have read his syndicated newspaper column and his monthly magazine, *Decision*. His movies have set a new pattern in the field of religious films.

Throughout his remarkable career, Dr. Graham has continually given credit for the good he has achieved to the God whom he serves.

Books by Billy Graham

My Answer
Peace with God
The Secret of Happiness
World Aflame

Published by POCKET BOOKS

PEACE
WITH
GOD

by Billy Graham

PUBLISHED BY POCKET BOOKS NEW YORK

PEACE WITH GOD

Doubleday edition published 1953

POCKET BOOK edition published April, 1965

54th printing...................September, 1976

This POCKET BOOK edition includes every word contained in
the original, higher-priced edition. It is printed from brand-
new plates made from completely reset, clear, easy-to-read type.
POCKET BOOK editions are published by
POCKET BOOKS,
a division of Simon & Schuster, Inc.,
A GULF+WESTERN COMPANY
630 Fifth Avenue,
New York, N.Y. 10020.
Trademarks registered in the United States
and other countries.

ISBN: 0-671-80758-7.
Printed in the U.S.A.

Dedicated to
L. NELSON BELL, M.D.
Surgeon, missionary statesman, editor,
adviser, and my close friend and father-in-law.

PREFACE

Many writers of religious books direct themselves to other religious writers or to theologians. Only on rare occasions do religious books appeal to the masses of ordinary men and women. This book has been written not for the theologians and philosophers but for the man in the street. My purpose is to give him a clear understanding of a new way of life that was presented by an unknown Galilean two thousand years ago. I have endeavored to present it in the language of the common man, that "the wayfaring men, though fools, shall not err therein."

I have tried to avoid those controversial subjects that have so often divided great segments of the Christian Church from each other—but, on the other hand, I have not bargained, parleyed, or compromised my concept of the Christian faith.

I am convinced that there is a great hunger of mind and thirst of soul on the part of the average man for peace with God.

I am aware that this book will be criticized by some and perhaps applauded by others. The modern-day pharisees who draw their self-righteous robes around them will not like it; but neither will the modern-day sadducees who deny the foundations of our belief—this is purely intentional on my part. We have pussyfooted, long enough in our religion. With the advent of the hydrogen bomb and the possibility of the cobalt bomb, we must come to grips with the issues of our day. We must face the realities as they are.

Those of you who are looking for a denomination to join will find no help in this book. I suggest you try some other shop. My object is not to get you to a particular denomination or church—but to get you to a saving knowledge of the Lord Jesus Christ, and to encourage, strengthen, and build up the Christian in the most holy faith.

In one sense, *Peace with God* has been years in the preparing. In another sense, it was done in a few hasty and hectic weeks. Continually there was the burning conviction that the American people needed just such a book.

Many ideas expressed in this book are not original with me—they have been picked up here and there across the years. If a quotation has been made and due credit not given, it is because the source has long since been forgotten and only the burning, convicting message of it remains.

Peace with God has literally been prepared on our knees. We have felt the continual presence of God. My daily prayer will be that in this hour of confusion and crisis, this book will be used to bring you to peace with God.

I am deeply grateful to all those who have counseled with me in the preparing of *Peace with God,* and have read the manuscript and made many helpful suggestions. Special thanks are due to: The Bishop of Barking, Church of England; Dr. Donald Grey Barnhouse, Dr. Robert O. Ferm, Mr. Mark Lee, Dr. Ralph W. Mitchell, Dr. Harold John Ockenga, Dr. Cecil Thompson, Dr. John S. Wimbish.

I also wish to thank Luverne Gustavson for her patient typing and retyping of the manuscript.

And I particularly wish to thank my loyal and faithful wife, who has read and reread the manuscript.

CONTENTS

PREFACE   vii

Part One: The Problem

1. THE QUEST   3
2. THE BIBLE   13
3. GOD   22
4. SIN   32
5. THE DEVIL   45
6. AFTER DEATH—WHAT?   56

Part Two: The Solution

7. WHY JESUS CAME   73
8. HOW AND WHERE TO BEGIN   91
9. REPENT   100
10. FAITH   108
11. THE NEW BIRTH   120
12. HOW TO BE SURE   129

Part Three: The Results

13. ENEMIES OF THE CHRISTIAN   139
14. RULES OF THE CHRISTIAN LIFE   150
15. THE CHRISTIAN AND THE CHURCH   160
16. SOCIAL OBLIGATIONS OF THE CHRISTIAN   173
17. THE FUTURE OF THE CHRISTIAN   190
18. PEACE—AT LAST   204

PART ONE: THE PROBLEM

Chapter One

THE QUEST

*And ye shall seek me, and find me, when ye shall
search for me with all your heart.*

JEREMIAH 29:13.

YOU started on the Great Quest the moment you were
born. It was many years perhaps before you realized it,
before it became apparent that you were constantly
searching—searching for something you never had—
searching for something that was more important than
anything in life. Sometimes you have tried to forget about
it. Sometimes you have attempted to lose yourself in
other things so there could be time and thought for nothing but the business at hand. Sometimes you may even
have felt that you were freed from the need to go on
seeking this nameless thing. At moments you have almost
been able to dismiss the quest completely. But always
you have been caught up in it again—always you have
had to come back to your search.

At the loneliest moments in your life you have looked
at other men and women and wondered if they too were
seeking—seeking something they couldn't describe but
knew they wanted and needed. Some of them seemed so
much happier and less burdened than you. Some of them
seemed to have found fulfillment in marriage and family
living. Others went off to achieve fame and wealth in
other parts of the world. Still others stayed at home and
prospered, and looking at them you may have thought:
"These people are not on the Great Quest. These people

have found their way. They knew what they wanted and
have been able to grasp it. It is only I who travel this
path that leads to nowhere. It is only I who go asking,
seeking, stumbling along this dark and despairing road
that has no guideposts."

But you are not alone. All mankind is traveling with
you, for all mankind is on this same quest. All humanity
is seeking the answer to the confusion, the moral sickness,
the spiritual emptiness that oppresses the world. All mankind is crying out for guidance, for comfort, for peace.

We are told that we live in the "age of anxiety." Historians point out that there have been few times in all
history when man has been subject to so much fear and
uncertainty. All the familiar props seem to have been
swept away. We talk of peace but are confronted by war.
We devise elaborate schemes for security but have not
found it. We grasp at every passing straw and even as
we clutch, it disappears.

For generations we have been running like frightened
children, up first one blind alley and then another. Each
time we have told ourselves: "This path is the right one,
this one will take us where we want to go." But each time
we have been wrong.

One of the first paths we chose was labeled "political
freedom." Give everyone political freedom, we said, and
the world will become a happy place. Let us select our
own government leaders and we shall have the kind of
government that will make life worth living. So we
achieved political freedom, but we did not achieve our
better world. Our daily newspapers give us reports of
corruption in high places, of favoritism, of exploitation,
of hypocrisy equal to and sometimes surpassing the des-
potism of ancient kings. Political freedom is a precious
and important thing, but it alone cannot give us the kind
of world we long for.

There was another very hopeful path marked "education," and many put their whole faith in it. Political freedom coupled with education will do the trick, they said,
and we all rushed madly along the educational path. It
seemed a bright, well-lighted, sensible path for a long

time, and we traveled it with eager, expectant feet, but where has it led us? You know the answer. We are the most informed people in the history of civilization—and yet the most miserable. Our high school students know more about the physical laws of the universe than the greatest scientist in the days of Aristotle. But though our heads are crammed with knowledge, our hearts are empty.

The brightest, most inviting path of all was the one marked "higher standards of living." Almost everyone felt he could trust this one to carry him automatically into that better and more joyful world. This was felt to be the sure route. This was the "press the button and you're there" route! This was the path that led through the beautiful full-color magazine advertisements, past all the shining new cars, past the gleaming rows of electric refrigerators and automatic washing machines, past all the fat chickens cooking in brand-new copper-bottomed pots. We knew we'd hit the jackpot this time! The other paths might have been false leads, but this time we had it!

All right, look around you right this minute. At this very moment in history you see in America a country that has political freedom to an extent that is undreamed of in many parts of the civilized world. You see the greatest and most far-reaching public education system that man has ever created, and we are eulogized at home and abroad for our high standard of living. "The American way of life" we like to call this fully electrified, fully automatic, chrome-plated economy of ours—but has it made us happy? Has it brought us the joy and satisfaction and the reason for living that we were seeking?

No. As we stand here feeling smug and proud that we have accomplished so much that generations before us only dreamed about; as we span our oceans in hours instead of months; as we produce miracle drugs that wipe out some of man's most dread diseases; as we erect buildings that make the Tower of Babel seem an anthill; as we learn more and more of the mysterious secrets that lie in the depths of the sea, and peer further and further into outer space, do we lose one iota of that empty feeling within us? Do all these modern wonders bring us a sense of fulfillment, do they help to explain why we are here, do they point out what we are supposed to learn?

Or does that awful hollow feeling persist? Does every further discovery of the magnitude of the universe comfort you or make you feel more alone and helpless than ever? Does the antidote for human fear and hatred and corruption lie in some laboratory test tube, or in an astronomer's telescope?

We cannot deny that science has given man many things he thought he wanted. But this same science has now presented us the most dreaded gift ever bestowed upon humanity. The life and future of every living being on this planet is affected by this gift of science. It stands like a somber shadow behind our waking thoughts. It stalks like a specter of horror through our children's dreams. We pretend it isn't there. We try to pretend that we haven't received this gift, that it's all a joke, and that some morning we'll wake up and find that the H-bomb hasn't really been invented and that the A-bomb has never been made—but our morning newspaper tells us different.

There are other paths, of course, and many are traveling them this very moment. There are the paths of fame and fortune, of pleasure and power. None of them leads anywhere but deeper into the mire. We are ensnared in the web of our own thinking, trapped so cleverly and so completely that we can no longer see either the cause or the cure of the disease that is inflicting such deadly pain.

If it is true that "for every illness there is a cure," then we must make haste to find it. The sand in civilization's hourglass is rapidly falling away, and if there is a path that leads to the light, if there is a way back to spiritual health, we must not lose an hour!

Many are floundering in this time of crisis and finding that their efforts are leading them not up but only further down into the pit. Last year the American people spent one hundred and twenty-five million dollars on fortune-tellers alone! One hundred and twenty-five million dollars given by frantic, frightened men and women to equally misguided people, to tell them the wrong answers to their pleading questions!

Last year over sixteen thousand Americans, who couldn't find even the wrong answers, took their own lives in preference to wandering any further in this man-made jungle we call civilization.

So. "Where are we?" you ask. "Where are we now and where are we going?" Let me tell you *where* we are and *what* we are. We are a nation of empty people. Our heads are crammed full of knowledge, but within our souls is a spiritual vacuum.

We complain that the youth of this country has lost its drive, its push, its willingness to work and to get ahead. Every day I hear parents say that they don't know what's the matter with their children—they don't want to make an effort, they just want everything handed to them. Parents don't seem to realize that their well-educated, carefully brought up children are actually empty inside. They aren't filled with the spirit that makes work a joy. They aren't filled with the determination that makes pushing ahead a pleasure. And why are they so empty? Because they don't know where they've come from, why they're here, or where they're going!

They are like rows of beautiful new automobiles, perfect in every detail but with no gasoline in the tanks. The exteriors are fine, but there's nothing inside to give them power. And so they just sit and rust—rust with boredom.

America is said to have the highest per capita boredom of any spot on earth! We know that because we have the greatest variety and greatest number of artificial amusements of any country. People have become so empty that they can't even entertain themselves. They have to pay other people to amuse them, to make them laugh, to try to make them feel warm and happy and comfortable for a few minutes, to try to lose that awful, frightening, hollow feeling—that terrible, dreaded feeling of being lost and alone.

You may think that boredom is a minor matter. Everyone gets bored sometimes, it's only natural. But let me tell you something about boredom, and this dangerous apathy that is creeping over the land and over the minds and hearts of the people. Man is the only one of God's creatures who is capable of being bored. No other living thing except man can ever be bored with itself or its surroundings. This is very significant, for the Creator never does anything without a purpose, and if He gave man the capacity for boredom, He did it for a purpose.

Boredom is one of the sure ways to measure your own inner emptiness! It's as accurate as a thermometer for telling just how hollow your inner spirit really is. The person who is thoroughly bored is living and working in a vacuum. His inner self is a vacuum, and there is nothing that nature resents more than a vacuum. It is one of the unfailing rules of this universe that all vacuums must be filled, and filled immediately.

We do not have to go back to ancient times to see what happens to a nation of empty people. We need look no further than the recent history of Germany, Italy, and Russia to see with what deadly speed nature fills up the vacuums that occur within us. Fascism and Communism can find no place in the heart and soul of a person who is filled with the Spirit of God, but it floods with the greatest ease into the minds and hearts of those who are empty and waiting. Nature abhors a vacuum, but it is up to us as individuals to determine with what our inner vacuums shall be filled.

So that is where we stand today—a nation of empty people. We have tried to fill ourselves with science and education, with better living and pleasure, with the many other things we thought we wanted, but we are still empty. Why are we empty? Because the Creator made us for Himself; and we shall never find completeness and fullness apart from fellowship with Him.

Jesus told us long ago that "Man shall not live by bread alone," [1] but we have paid no heed. We have gone on stuffing ourselves with bread of every description. We have stuffed until we are sick.

We cannot stand the terrible emptiness of ourselves,

[1] *Luke 4:4.*

we cannot look at the lonely desolate road that lies ahead. We are desperately weary of the hatred and greed and lust that we know are within us, but we are helpless to be rid of it and filled with something better.

Time is of the essence. The tools of total annihilation have been placed within our reach. We cannot scurry up any more false paths, we cannot explore any more unknown roads, we cannot afford to be trapped in any more blind alleys. We don't have that much time! For our generation has accomplished what other generations only *tried* to do, or dreamed of doing in their most insane moments of power and ruthlessness! We have achieved a weapon of total destruction. We are witnessing the climax of man's madness—the atom cleaved!

How the demons must have laughed as some of the most brilliant men on earth worked furiously for years to achieve this horror! The atom cleaved! Divide and conquer! Split apart, destroy, shatter, crush, crumble! He of the cloven hoof has done his work, and men have been avid to aid him. We see before us Satan's masterpiece, his clever counterfeit of the cloven tongues of divine fire. For this satanic fire and the pentecostal flames both fall from above, both are cloven, both illuminate, both instantly transform everything they touch—but with such a difference. The difference of heaven and hell!

We are living in a topsy-turvy world, where all is confusion. But you may be sure that it is confusion with a plan—Satan's plan! The Bible tells us that Satan is the great deceiver and he has devoted himself to the cause of our great self-deception and to the deceptions that lie between nations all over this world. He has led us to believe that things were getting better, when they are really getting worse.

The brilliant English scholar, Dr. Henry Bett, says, "The easygoing optimism of the 90's, when it was almost taken for granted that the world was automatically progressing toward perfection, is impossible today. The vague notion that education, and humanitarianism and 'progress' were gradually and inevitably leading to a kind of utopia, has been pretty well disproved by the events

of the past twenty-five years. Things are not as easy as all
that. Satan is not dead. The principalities and powers of
darkness are still alive and the whole world still lieth in
the Evil One."

We all recognize that the world has changed radically
since the beginning of this century. We are aware of its
increased tempo, of the spirit of revolution that is sweep-
ing away the established landmarks and traditions, of the
speed with which language, fashions, customs, housing,
and our ways of living and thinking are being altered and
changed.

Only a few years ago children were delighted at the
prospect of a trip to the wharves to see the great ships
come in. Today they are blasé about helicopters and jet
planes. We who once marveled at the telegraph, now
take the far greater miracle of television for granted. Not
so long ago many of man's physical diseases were termed
hopeless and incurable. Today, we have drugs so effective
that many old-age diseases are becoming rare. We have
accomplished much, of that there is no doubt.

But with all this progress, man has not solved the basic
problem of the human race. We can build the highest
buildings, the fastest ships, the longest bridges—but we
still can't govern ourselves or live together in equality
and peace!

We may create vast new schools of art and music, we
may discover newer and better vitamins, but there is
nothing new about our troubles. They are the same old
ones that man has always had, only they seem magnified
and more abundant. They may come upon us in new
ways, they may seem to give sharper pain and deeper
anguish; but fundamentally we are facing the same temptations, the same trials, the same testings that have always
confronted mankind.

For ever since that tragic moment in the Garden of
Eden, when man gave up God's will for his own will,
man has been plagued by the same problems. Their cause
is stated in the first chapter of Genesis. The terrible conditions that produced them are related in the first chapter

of Romans. And the gospel of Jesus Chirst gives us their remedy.

It is man's depraved and sinful nature that fills him with hate, envy, greed, and jealousy. The curse of sin is upon his body and he is forever haunted by the fear of death. His inventive genius has enabled him to change everything but himself. For man, in spite of the loudly acclaimed "progress" of our times, remains just as he was in the beginning.

Sin, too, has remained unchanged, although man has done his best to alter it. We've tried to dress it up with other names. We've put new labels on the same old bottle of poison. We've tired to whitewash the old barn and pretend it was another building.

We've tried calling sins "errors" or "mistakes" or "poor judgment," but sin itself has stayed the same. No matter how we try to salve our conscience, we've known all along that men are still sinners; and the results of sin are still disease, disappointment, disillusionment, despair, and death.

Sorrow hasn't changed, either. It began when Adam and Eve looked with broken hearts upon the lifeless body of their murdered son Abel and knew the crushing weight of grief. It has gone on, until today sorrow is the universal language of man. No one escapes it, everyone experiences it. It even seemed to one of Job's comforters that it was the aim of life, for he said, "Yet man is born unto trouble, as the sparks fly upward." [2]

Death is also still the same. Men have tried to change its appearance. We have changed the word "undertaker" to "mortician." We place bodies in "caskets" now instead of "coffins." We have "funeral homes" instead of "undertaking parlors" and "memorial parks" instead of "cemeteries." We try to soften the starkness of the last rites; but regardless of what we call it, or how we rouge the cheeks, the cold, hard, cruel reality of death has not changed throughout all of man's history.

These three facts constitute the true story of man: his

[2] Job 5:7.

past is filled with sin; his present is overflowing with sorrow; and the certainty of death faces him in the future.

The Bible says, "It is appointed unto men once to die," [3] and to the average person this seems a stark and hopeless situation. Hundreds of philosophies and scores of religions have been invented by men in their efforts to circumvent the Word of God. Modern philosophers and psychologists are still trying to make it appear that there is some way out other than the path of Jesus. But man has tried them all and none of them leads anywhere but down.

Christ came to give us the answers to the three enduring problems of sin, sorrow, and death. It is Jesus Christ, and He alone, who is also enduring and unchanging, "the same yesterday, and today and forever." [4]

All other things may change, but Christ remains unchangeable. In the restless sea of human passions, Christ stands steadfast and calm, ready to welcome all who will turn to Him and accept the blessings of safety and peace. For we are living in an age of grace, in which God promises that whosoever will may come and receive His Son. But this period of grace will not go on indefinitely. We are even now living on borrowed time.

[3] *Hebrews 9:27.*   [4] *Hebrews 13:8.*

Chapter Two

THE BIBLE

Heaven and earth shall pass away, but my words shall not pass away.

MATTHEW 24:35.

TIME is running out. The seconds are ticking away toward midnight. The human race is about to take the fatal plunge. Which way shall we turn? Is there any authority left? Is there a path we can follow? Is there any light penetrating the Stygian darkness? Can we find a codebook that will give us the key to our dilemmas? Is there any source of authority to which we can turn? Have we just been placed here by some unknown creator or force without any clue as to where we came from, why we are here, and where we are going?

The answer is, No. We do have a codebook. We do have a key. We do have authoritative source material. It is found in the ancient and historic Book we call the Bible. This Book has come down to us through the ages. It has passed through so many hands, appeared in so many forms—and survived attack of every kind. Neither barbaric vandalism nor civilized scholarship has touched it. Neither the burning of fire nor the laughter of skepticism has accomplished its annihilation. Through the many dark ages of man, its glorious promises have survived unchanged.

Now, as we approach what appears to be another decisive hour in world history, let us re-examine this indestructible Book of wisdom and prophecy; let us find out why this particular volume has endured and been man's unfailing source of faith and spiritual strength.

There are those who regard the Bible principally as the history of Israel. Others admit that it sets forth the soundest ethics ever enunciated. But these things, important as they are, are only incidental to the real theme of the Bible, which is the story of God's redemption as it exists in Jesus Christ. Those who read the Scriptures as magnificent literature, breathtaking poetry or history, and overlook the story of salvation, miss the Bible's real meaning and message.

God caused the Bible to be written for the express purpose of revealing to man God's plan for his redemption. God caused this Book to be written that He might make His everlasting laws clear to His children, and that they might have His great wisdom to guide them and His great love to comfort them as they make their way through life. For without the Bible, this world would indeed be a dark and frightening place, without signpost or beacon.

The Bible easily qualifies as the only book in which God's revelation is contained. There are many bibles of different religions; there is the Mohammedan Koran, the Buddhist Canon or Sacred Scripture, the Zoroastrian Zendavesta, and the Brahman Vedas. All of these have been made accessible to us by reliable translations, and we may judge of their value. It is soon discovered that all these non-Christian bibles are all developments in the wrong direction. They all begin with some flashes of true light and end in utter darkness. Even the most casual observer soon discovers that the Bible is radically different. It is the only Book that offers man a redemption and points the way out of his dilemmas.

Sixteen hundred years were needed to complete the writing of the Bible. It is the work of more than thirty authors, each of whom acted as a scribe to God. These men, many of whom lived generations apart, did not set down merely what they thought or hoped. They acted as channels for God's dictation; they wrote as He directed them; and under His divine inspiration they were able to see the great and enduring truths, and to record them that other men might see and know them too.

During these sixteen hundred years, the sixty-six books of the Bible were written by men of different languages, living in different times, and in different countries; but the message they wrote was one. God spoke to each man in his own language, in his own time, but His message basically in each case was the same. When the great scholars gathered together the many ancient manuscripts written in Hebrew, Aramaic and Greek, and translated them into a single modern tongue, they found that God's promises remain unchanged, His great message to man had not varied. As we read these ageless words today, we find that the rules of conduct set forth by the ancient scribes are as fresh and meaningful to this generation as they were to the people of Jesus' time.

It is small wonder, then, that the Bible has always been the world's best seller! No other book can touch its profound wisdom, its poetic beauty, or the accuracy of its history and prophecy. Its critics, who claimed it to be filled with forgery, fiction, and unfilled promises, are finding that the difficulties lie with themselves, and not the Bible. Greater and more careful scholarship has shown that apparent contradictions were caused by incorrect translations rather than divine inconsistencies. It was man and not the Bible that needed correcting.

And yet—in many homes and among so-called educated people—it has become fashionable to joke about the Bible and to regard it more as a dust catcher than as the living Word of God. When asked by her minister if she knew what was in the Bible, one little girl proudly replied that she knew everything that was in it, and proceeded to list "the picture of her sister's boy friend, the recipe for mother's favorite hand lotion, a lock of baby brother's hair, and the ticket for Pa's watch!" That was all she knew about the family Bible. Too many families have used the Bible as a safe storage place for old letters and pressed flowers, and have overlooked entirely the help and assurance that God intended this Book to give them.

This attitude is changing now, and changing fast! Life

is being stripped of its artificialities, its meaningless trimmings. The false promises that man has made to man are standing forth now as the glaring errors they are. As we cast our frightened eyes around for something that is real and true and enduring, we are turning once more to this ancient Book that has given consolation, comfort, and salvation to millions in the centuries past.

Yes, people are "discovering" the Bible again! They are dusting off their old copies or buying new ones. They are finding the familiar but almost forgotten phrases ring with a current meaning that makes them seem to have been written only yesterday. This is because the Bible embodies all the knowledge man needs to fill the longing of his soul and solve all his problems. It is the blueprint of the Master Architect, and only by following its directions can we build the life we are seeking.

Here in America we have another great document that we value and respect. It was written almost one hundred and fifty years ago by a number of men who labored long and debated even longer over its many provisions, and finally sent it to the thirteen federated states for ratification. The men who framed our Constitution knew they were writing the basic document for a government of free men: they recognized that men could live as free and independent beings only if each one knew and understood the law. They were to know their rights, their privileges, and their limitations. They were to stand as equals before the court of law and few judges could be unfair; for the judge, too, was bound by the same law and required to try each case accordingly.

While the rest of the world watched this great human experiment, men found that if they knew the law and lived according to it, they could, in truth, be free! A man could know just where he stood. He had his Constitutional rights and he also had his Constitutional responsibilities. If he neglected one, the other would suffer—as so many negligent voters who came later were to discover when they found themselves saddled with governmental restrictions they didn't like!

Just as America has grown and prospered within the

framework of our Constitution, so Christianity has flourished and spread according to the laws set forth in the Bible. Just as the Constitution was intended to apply equally to all men living under it, without special favor or interpretation, so the Bible stands as the supreme Constitution for all mankind, its laws applying equally to all who live under its domain, without exception or special interpretation.

As the Constitution is the highest law of the land, so the Bible is the highest law of God. For it is in the Bible that God sets forth His spiritual laws. It is in the Bible that God makes His enduring promises. It is in the Bible that God reveals the plan of redemption for the human race.

In the wonders of nature we see God's laws in operation. Who has not looked up at the stars on a cloudless night, and marveled in silent awe at the glory of God's handiwork? Who has not felt his heart lifted in the spring of the year, as he sees all creation bursting with new life and vigor? In the beauty and abundance around us we see the magnitude of God's power and the infinite detail of His planning; but nature tells us nothing of God's love or God's grace. We do not find the promise of our personal salvation in nature.

Conscience tells us in our innermost being of the presence of God and of the moral difference between good and evil; but this is a fragmentary message, in no way as distinct and comprehensive as the lessons of the Bible. It is only in its pages that we find the clear and unmistakable message upon which all true Christianity is based.

Christianity finds all its doctrines stated in the Bible, and the true Christian denies no part, nor attempts to add anything to the Word of God. While the Constitution of the United States may be amended from time to time, no amendment is ever necessary for the Bible. We truly believe that the men who wrote the Bible were guided by the Holy Spirit, both in the thoughts they expressed and in their choice of words. As Peter said, "For the prophecy came not in old time by the will of man: but holy men of God spake as they were moved by the Holy Ghost." [1]

Paul tells us that "All scripture is given by inspiration of God, and is profitable for doctrine, for reproof, for correction, for instruction in righteousness: That the man of God may be perfect, thoroughly furnished unto all good works." [2]

In setting down their forthright messages, Biblical scribes have never attempted to gloss over the realities of life. The sins of the great and small are freely admitted, the weaknesses of human nature are acknowledged, and life in Biblical times is recorded as it was lived. The startling thing is that the lives and motivations of these people who lived so long ago have such a modern flavor! As we read, the pages seem like mirrors held up before our own minds and hearts, reflecting our prides and prejudices, our own failures and humiliations, our own sins and sorrows.

Truth is timeless. Truth does not differ from one age to another, from one people to another, from one geographical location to another. Men's ideas may differ, men's customs may change, men's moral codes may vary, but the great all-prevailing truth stands for time and eternity.

The message of Jesus Christ, our Savior, is the story of the Bible—it is the story of salvation. Profound students of the Bible have traced the story of Jesus Christ from the beginning of the Old Testament, for He is the true theme of the Old as well as the New Testament.

He appears in Genesis as the Seed of the Woman.

In Exodus, He is the Passover Lamb.

In Leviticus, He is the Atoning Sacrifice.

In Numbers, He is the Smitten Rock.

In Deuteronomy, He is the Prophet.

In Joshua, He is the Captain of the Lord's Hosts.

In Judges, He is the Deliverer.

In Ruth, He is the Heavenly Kinsman.

In the six books of Kings, He is the Promised King.

In Nehemiah, He is the Restorer of the nation.

[1] 2 Peter 1:21.   [2] 2 Timothy 3:16-17.

In Esther, He is the Advocate.

In Job, He is my Redeemer.

In Psalms, He is my All and in All.

In Proverbs, He is my Pattern.

In Ecclesiastes, He is my Goal.

In the Song of Solomon, He is my Satisfier.

In the Prophets, He is the Coming Prince of Peace.

In the Gospels, He is Christ coming to seek and to save.

In Acts, He is Christ risen.

In the Epistles, He is Christ at the Father's right hand.

In the Revelation, He is Christ returning and reigning.

This is the eternal message of the Bible. It is the story of life, peace, eternity, and heaven. The Bible has no hidden purpose. It has no need for special interpretation. It has a single, clear, bold message for every living being—the message of Christ and His offer of peace with God.

One day upon a mountain near Capernaum Jesus sat with His disciples. They gathered before Him. Perhaps Peter on one side and John on the other. Jesus may have looked quietly and tenderly at each of these devoted disciples, looked at them the way a loving parent looks at the members of his family—loving each child separately, loving each one for a special reason, loving them in such a way that each child feels singled out and individually embraced. That is how Jesus must have loved His disciples.

The little group must have become very reverent under His serene and loving gaze. They must have become very still within themselves with the feeling that something momentous was about to be said, something they must remember, something they must be able to transmit to others all over the world who were not privileged, as they were, to hear these words from the Master's own lips.

For there, on the mountain, standing perhaps under the silvery, gray-green leaves of an olive tree, Jesus preached the greatest sermon that human ears have ever heard. He explained the essence of Christian living. When he was through and a holy hush had settled on His wide-eyed listeners, they "were astonished at His doctrine: for

He taught them as one having authority, and not as the scribes." [3]

Indeed He did teach with authority, the authority of God Himself; and the rules He set forth were God's own rules, the ones which every Christian with the hope of salvation in his heart must follow.

If you do not have a Bible in your home, go out and get one now—get the one that suits you best, get the size that is most comfortable for you to handle, get the kind of type that is most pleasant for you to read, and then settle down and find out for yourself why this one Book has endured. Find out for yourself why it answers every human need, why it supplies the faith and strength that keeps humanity marching forward.

If you and the Bible have had a long absence from each other, it might be well for you to renew your acquaintance by reading again the Gospel of John. While this is considered one of the most profound books in the Bible, it is also the clearest and most readily understood. It was written for the very purpose of showing the *how* and the *why* of man's salvation, so that the questions of the mind as well as the gropings of the heart might be satisfied.

After reading the Book of John, you might acquaint yourself with the Gospel as taught by Mark, Luke, and Matthew, noting how these men of widely different personalities and writing styles set forth the eternal story of redemption through Jesus. You will become aware of the powerful, universal truth that underlies all Gospel teaching and be impressed anew with what Paul meant when he said, "Jesus Christ the same yesterday, and today, and forever." [4]

When you have read each of the Gospels individually, start in at the beginning of the New Testament and read straight through all the books in order. When you have done that, you will have developed such a taste for Bible reading, you will have found it such a fountain of inspiration, such a practical counselor and guide, such a

---

[3] *Matthew 7:28, 29.*   [4] *Hebrews 13:8.*

treasure chest of sound advice, that you will make Bible reading a part of your daily life.

A knowledge of the Bible is essential to a rich and meaningful life. For the words of this Book have a way of filling in the missing pieces, of bridging the gaps, of turning the tarnished colors of our life to jewel-like brilliance. Learn to take your every problem to the Bible. Within its pages you will find the correct answer.

But most of all, the Bible is a revelation of the nature of God. The philosophers of the centuries have struggled with the problem of a Supreme Being. Who is He? What is He? Where is He? If there is such a Person, is He interested in me? If so, how can I know Him? These and a thousand other questions about God are revealed in this Holy Book we call the Bible.

Chapter Three

GOD

Canst thou by searching find out God?
JOB 11:7.

WHO is God? What is He like? How can we be sure He exists? When did He begin? Can we know Him?

Everyone has asked these questions either aloud or to himself, for we cannot look at the world around us and not wonder about its creation. We are daily faced with the miracle of life and the mystery of death, of the glory of flowering trees, the magnificence of the star-filled sky, the magnitude of mountains and of sea. Who made all this? Who conceived the law of gravity by which everything is held in its proper place? Who ordered the day and the night and the regular procession of the seasons?

The only possible answer is that all these things and many more are the work of a Supreme Creator. As a watch must have a designer, so our precision-like universe has a Great Designer. We call Him God. His is a name with whom the whole human race is familiar. From earliest childhood we have breathed His name. The Bible declares that the God we talk about, the God we sing about, the God "from whom all blessings flow!" is the God who created this world and placed us in it.

But "Who is He?" you ask. "Where is He?" We all know His name. We call upon Him in our hours of greatest difficulty and trial. Many of us try to let the thought of Him fill our every waking moment. Others say

22

they don't believe in Him, that He doesn't exist. And still others say, "Explain Him to me and maybe I'll accept God."

If that is how you feel, if all your life you have been hearing about God and talking about God, but waiting for someone to explain God to you before you could put your faith in Him, and Him alone, let us see just how concrete a description the Bible can give us.

At this crucial point in world history, everyone should be seeking an answer to the question, "What is God like?" Everyone should ask it, and everyone should make very sure of the answer. Everyone should know beyond a shadow of a doubt exactly who God is and what He is capable of accomplishing.

It is the absence of the knowledge of God and man's refusal to obey Him that lies at the root of every problem that besets us. It is man's confusion about God's plan that has the world in chaos. It is man's unwillingness to learn and to obey God's laws that has laid such a heavy burden on our soul. So let us learn all that we can about Him.

Where shall we go for this knowledge? Who among us can tell us the truth? Are we not all finite creatures here together? Has God designated any one person here on earth to speak with final authority about Him? No— the one man who could do that lived two thousand years ago, and we crucified Him! How, then, are we to find out?

We can ask the learned scholars, and they may tell us that God is the expression of everything that is in nature and life, that all living beings are one with God, that life itself is an expression of His Divine Being. They will tell you that you can see God in the tiniest drop of water and in the great arch in the sky above.

Ask a philosopher, and he will tell you that God is the original and immutable force behind all creation, that He is the Master Dynamo that keeps all the worlds in motion —that He is the Power without beginning or end. The philosopher will say that every bit of life and beauty that we see is a manifestation of this power that flows in an unending current out from the Dynamo and back again.

Ask still further and you may be told that God is absolute, that He is All in All, and that no one can possibly know any more about Him. There are many different definitions for God. Every country, every race of people, every family, every individual has tried to explain the Great Being behind the universe. Men of all ages have tried to discover the Creator whose work they saw, but whom they knew not. Which of these varied explanations is right? Which of these many theories are we to accept? By which of these self-appointed authorities are we to be guided?

As we have already seen in our previous chapter, God has revealed Himself in the Book we call the Bible. If we believe that in the Bible we have a revelation of God, then our minds can be completely satisfied and our hearts completely filled. We can rest assured that we have the correct answer, that we are on our way to knowing and understanding the true nature of God.

God reveals Himself in hundreds of ways in the Bible, and if we read the Bible as carefully and as regularly as we read the daily papers, we would be as familiar with and as well informed about God as we are about our favorite player's batting average during baseball season!

As a diamond has many facets, so there are innumerable aspects of God's revelation of Himself which would take volumes to fill. Suffice it to say, with our limited space we can cover four aspects of God's revelation of Himself which seem to be the most significant, and which we should carry with us always.

First: the Bible declares God to be *Spirit*. Jesus talking to the woman at the Well of Sychar made this straightforward statement about God: "God is Spirit." [1]

What do you think of when you hear the word *spirit*? What mental image does it bring to your mind? Do you think of a wisp of vapor drifting across the sky? Does *spirit* mean the sort of thing that frightens children on Halloween? Is *spirit* just a formless nothingness to you?

[1] John 4:24.

Do you think that was what Jesus meant when He said, "God is Spirit"?

To discover what "spirit" really is, and what Jesus meant when He used that particular word, we must turn again to the Bible to the scene where Christ after His resurrection says: "Handle Me, and see; for a spirit hath not flesh and bones, as ye see Me have." [2] Therefore we can be sure that spirit is *without* body. It is the exact *opposite* of body. Yet it has being and power. This is difficult for us to understand because we are trying to understand it with finite, body-limited minds.

As human beings deprived of the unlimited vision that God originally intended His creatures to have, we cannot comprehend the glory and the magnitude of the Spirit that lies so far outside ourselves. When we hear the word "spirit," we immediately try to reduce it to our puny size, to make it fit within the scope of our small minds. It is like trying to explain the sweep and majesty and awe-inspiring grandeur of the ocean to a person who has never seen a body of water larger than a mud puddle! How can such a person envision the boundless sea? How can such a person, looking into a shallow, murky pool, fathom the bottomless depths, the mysterious life, the surging power, the ceaseless roll, the terrible ruthlessness of ocean storm or the all-surpassing beauty of ocean calm? How could anyone who had looked only into a mud puddle know what you were talking about? What word could you use to give a convincing picture of the mighty sea? How could you make him believe that such a wonder really exists?

How infinitely more difficult it is for us to grasp what Jesus meant when He said: "God is Spirit." Jesus knew! His mind was not limited as ours are limited. His eyes were not focused on the mud puddle of life. He knew full well the borderless reaches of the Spirit, and He came to try to give us some understanding of its wonders, its comfort, and its peace.

We do know that the spirit is not something that is

[2] *Luke* 24:39.

bound in a body. Spirit is not wearable as a body. Spirit is not changeable as a body. The Bible declares that God is such a Spirit—that He is not limited to body; He is not limited to shape; He is not limited to boundaries or bonds; He is absolutely immeasurable and undiscernible by eyes that can see only physical things. The Bible tells us that because He has no such limitations He can be everywhere at once, that He can hear all, see all, and know all.

We can't do that, and so we try to limit God as we are limited. We try to deny God the power to do things we can't do. We try to say that because we can't be everywhere at once, God can't be, either! We are rather like the person who, having heard about the ocean, finally makes his way to the beach one day and going down to the edge of the water, scoops up a few drops and holds them in his hands.

"Ah," he exclaims, "at last I have made the ocean mine! I hold the ocean in my hands, I possess it!" True, he does have a part of the ocean, but at the same moment other people on a thousand other shores may be reaching down and claiming a few drops of the ocean for themselves. The world's millions could come down to the beach and reach out their hands to be filled with sea water. They could each take as much as they wanted, as much as they needed—and still the ocean would remain unchanged. Its mightiness and power would be the same, the life in its unfathomable depths would continue unaltered, although it had supplied the needs of every single person standing with outstretched hands along its many shores.

So it is with God. He can be everywhere at once, heeding the prayers of all who call out in the name of Christ; performing the mighty miracles that keep the stars in their places and the plants bursting up through the earth and the fish swimming in the sea. There is no limit to God. There is no limit to His wisdom. There is no limit to His power. There is no limit to His love. There is no limit to His mercy.

If you have been trying to limit God—stop it! Don't try to confine Him or His works to any single place or sphere.

You wouldn't try to limit the ocean. You wouldn't be bold enough to try to change the course of the moon, or to stop the earth as it turns on its axis! How everlastingly more foolish it is to try to limit the God who created and controls all these wonders!

I am eternally grateful to my mother for many things, but one of the most enduring blessings she brought into my life was to teach me at the age of ten that "God is a Spirit, Infinite, Eternal, and Unchangeable." That definition of God has been with me all my life, and when a man knows in his heart that God is an Infinite, Eternal, and Unchanging Spirit, it helps to overcome the temptation to limit Him. It helps to overcome all doubt about His ability to accomplish things that you can't do yourself!

Some who doubt that the Bible is the true Word of God, doubt it because they are unwilling to ascribe to God anything they cannot themselves achieve. If you have any uncertainty about the inspiration of the Bible, go back and look at it again. Look at it in the light of a person who has been staring at a mud puddle all his life, and who is confronted for the first time by a view of the ocean! Perhaps you are only now catching your first glimpse of God's unlimited power. Perhaps you are only now beginning to understand Him for what He actually is. For if God is the Spirit that Jesus declares Him to be, there is no problem of providence, there is no problem of His sovereignty in the affairs of men, there is no problem of His inspiration of the men who wrote the Bible. Everything fits into place once you understand who and what God really is.

Second: the Bible reveals Him as a *Person*. All through the Bible it says: "God loves," "God says," "God does." Everything that we attribute to a person is attributed to God. A person is one who feels, thinks, wishes, desires, and has all the expressions of personality.

Here on earth we confine personality to the body. Our finite minds cannot envision personality that is not manifested through flesh and bones. We know that our own personalities will not always be clothed in the bodies they now inhabit. We know that at the moment of death our personalities will leave our bodies and go on to the destinations that await them. We know all this—yet it is difficult for us to accept it.

What a revelation if we could all realize that personality does not have to be identified with a physical being. God is not bound by a body, yet He is a Person. He feels, He thinks, He loves, He forgives, He sympathizes with the problems and sorrows that we face.

Third: the Bible states that God is not only a Spirit and a Person, but God is a *Holy and Righteous Being*. From Genesis to Revelation, God reveals Himself as a Holy God. He is utterly perfect and absolute in every detail. He is too holy to touch sinful man, too holy to endure sinful living. He is a Holy and a Perfect God.

If we could envision the true picture of His majestic righteousness, what a difference it would make in the way we live as individuals and as nations! If we could once realize the tremendous gulf that separates unrighteous man from God's perfect righteousness, the world could be changed overnight! The Scripture declares Him to be the Light in whom there is no darkness at all—the one Supreme Being without flaw or blemish.

Here again is a difficult concept for imperfect man to understand. We, whose faults and weaknesses are everywhere apparent, can scarcely imagine the overwhelming holiness of God—but we must recognize it if we are to understand and benefit from the Bible.

The chasm that separates imperfect man from perfect God is emphasized all through the Scriptures. We see it in the division of the Tabernacle and the Temple into the Holy and Most Holy places. It is pointed out in the prescribed offering that must be brought if a sinner would approach God. It is underscored by a special priesthood to mediate between God and the people. It was emphasized by the laws concerning impurity in the Book of Leviticus. We see it in the many feasts of Israel, by the isolation of Israel in Palestine. The Holiness of God regulates all other principles of God.

The Scripture declares that His throne is established

on the basis of His holiness. It is because God is holy and
man is unholy that so wide a rift exists between God and
the unrepentant sinner. The Bible tells us that our iniquities have separated us from God—separated us so
completely that His face is hidden from us and He will
not hear us when we call.

For God is too pure to look with approval upon evil.
He is too holy to have any traffic with sin. Before sin
entered into the human race, God and man had fellowship with each other. Now that fellowship is broken, and
all communication between God and man is lost outside
of Jesus Christ. It is only through Jesus Christ that man
can ever again re-establish His fellowship with God.

Man by himself is a sinner, powerless to change his
position, powerless to reach the pure ear of God with his
own sinful tongue. Man would have remained forever
lost if God in His infinite mercy had not sent His Son
to earth to bridge this gulf.

It is in God's holiness that we find the reason for the
death of Christ. His holiness demanded the most exacting
penalty for sin, and His love provided Jesus Christ to pay
this penalty and provide man with salvation. Because the
God we worship is a pure God, a holy God, a just and
righteous God, He sent us His only begotten Son to make
it possible for us to have access to Him. But if we ignore
the help He has sent, if we fail to obey the laws He has
set forth, we cannot cry out to Him for mercy when the
punishment we deserve falls upon us!

Fourth: *God is Love.* But as with the other attributes
of God, many persons who do not read their Bibles fail
to recognize what is meant when the Scriptures say: "God
is love." [3]

We aren't always sure ourselves what we mean when
we use the term *love.* That word has become one of the
most widely misused words in our language. We use the
word *love* to describe the basest as well as the most
exalted of human relationships. We say we "love" to
travel; we "love" to eat chocolate cake; we "love" our new

[3] *John 4:8.*

car, or the pattern in the wallpaper in our home. Why, we even say we "love" our neighbors—but most of us don't do much more than just say it and let it go at that! No wonder we don't have a very clear idea of what the Bible means when it says: "God is Love."

Don't make the mistake of thinking that because God is Love that everything is going to be sweet, beautiful, and happy and that no one will be punished for his sins. God's holiness demands that all sin be punished, but God's love provides the plan and way of redemption for sinful man. God's love provided the cross of Jesus, by which man can have forgiveness and cleansing. It was the love of God that sent Jesus Christ to the cross!

Never question God's great love, for it is as unchangeable a part of God as is His holiness. No matter how black your sins, God loves you. Were it not for the love of God, none of us would ever have a chance in the future life. But God is Love! And His love for us is everlasting! "But God commendeth His love toward us, in that while we were yet sinners, Christ died for us." [4]

The promises of God's love and forgiveness are as real, as sure, as positive as human words can make them. But like describing the ocean, its total beauty cannot be understood until it is actually seen. It is the same with God's love. Until you actually accept it, until you actually experience it, until you actually possess true peace with God, no one can describe its wonders to you.

It is not something that you do with your mind. Your finite mind is not capable of dealing with anything as great as the love of God. Your mind might have difficulty explaining how a black cow can eat green grass and give white milk—but you drink the milk and are nourished by it. Your mind can't reason through all the intricate processes that take place when you plant a small flat seed that produces a huge vine bearing luscious red and green watermelons—but you eat them and enjoy them! Your mind can't explain the electricity that may be creating the light by which you are reading at this very moment—

[4] *Romans* 5:8.

but you know that it's there and that it is making it possible for you to read!

You have to receive God by faith—by faith in His Son, the Lord Jesus Christ. And when that happens, there isn't any room for doubt. You don't have to question whether or not God is in your heart, you can know it.

Whenever anyone asks me how I can be so certain about who and what God really is, I am reminded of the story of the little boy who was out flying a kite. It was a fine day for kite flying, the wind was brisk and large billowy clouds were blowing across the sky. The kite went up and up until it was entirely hidden by the clouds.

"What are you doing?" a man asked the little boy.

"I'm flying a kite," he replied.

"Flying a kite, are you?" the man said. "How can you be sure? You can't see your kite."

"No," said the boy, "I can't see it, but every little while I feel a tug, so I know for sure that it's there!"

Don't take anyone else's word for God. Find Him for yourself, and then you too will know by the wonderful, warm tug on your heartstrings that He is there *for sure*.

Chapter Four

SIN

For all have sinned, and come short of the glory of God.

ROMANS 3:23.

IF GOD is a righteous and loving Being, why then is there so much wickedness, suffering and sorrow? How did all this hatred come to be? Why have we created false idols? Why do we worship at the shrines of war and greed and self-interest? How did the human race, which God made in His own image, sink so deep into depravity that the Ten Commandments had to be set forth with the demand that they be kept? Why did God have to send His own Son to save us? How did God's creatures become so filled with lust and evil?

To understand it, to see clearly why nation is pitted against nation, why families are divided, why every newspaper is filled with reports of violent, insane acts of brutality and hate, we must go back to the very beginning. We must go back to the story of Adam in the Garden, back to the first chapter of Genesis.

Some people say that this familiar story of creation is only a myth. They say it is but a simple way to explain an unanswerable question to children. But this is not so. The Bible tells us exactly what happened in the beginning and why man has moved steadily along the path of his own destruction ever since.

For God created this world as a perfect whole. He created the beautiful, harmonious world that man threw away—the perfect world that we are longing to find again, the world for which we are all searching.

In this perfect world God placed a perfect man. Adam was perfect because nothing that God does can ever be less than perfect, and upon this perfect man God bestowed the most precious of all gifts—the gift of freedom. God gave to man the freedom of choice.

The first man was no cave dweller—no jibbering, grunting, growling creature of the forest trying to subdue the perils of the jungle and the beasts of the field. Adam was created full-grown with every mental and physical faculty developed. He walked with God and had fellowship with Him. He was intended to be as a king on earth, ruling by the will of God.

This, then, was Adam's position as he stood in the Garden, the perfect man, the first man, and the only earthly creature to whom God had ever given the priceless gift of freedom. Adam had *total* freedom—freedom to choose or to reject, freedom to obey God's commands or to go contrary to them, freedom to make himself happy or miserable. For it is not the mere possession of freedom that makes life satisfying—it is what we choose to *do* with our freedom that determines whether or not we shall find peace with ourselves and with God.

This is the real heart of the problem, for the moment a man is given freedom he is faced by two paths. Freedom is meaningless if there is only one possible path to follow. Freedom implies the right to choose, to select, to determine one's individual course of action.

We all know men and women who are honest, not so much from free choice, but because they have no opportunity to be dishonest. We all know people who pride themselves on being good, when it is actually their surroundings and way of life that keep them from being bad. We cannot take credit for resisting temptation if no temptation is placed before us!

God gave Adam no such handicap. He granted him freedom of choice and He gave him every opportunity to exercise it. Because God could do nothing that was less than perfect, He provided Adam with the perfect

setting in which to prove whether or not he would serve
God.

As Adam stood there in the Garden he was without
sin, his innocence was without blemish. The whole universe lay before him. The as yet unwritten history of the
human race stretched like a great sheet of purest parch-
ment beneath his hand, waiting for him to write the opening chapter—waiting for him to determine which road
future generations would take.

God had completed His work. He had created an
earthly garden, rich in everything that man might need.
He had created a perfect man in His own likeness. He
had endowed this man with a mind and a soul, and given
him complete freedom to use his mind and to dispose of
his soul as he saw fit. Then, like the wise Parent that He
was, God waited to see what choice this child of His
would make.

This was the test! This was the moment when Adam
would use his free will to choose the right path or the
wrong path—choose it because he *wanted* to, and not because there was only one path open to him!

He made his choice. He suffered the consequences of
it, and he set the pattern that all humanity was to follow.
"Therefore, as by the offence of one, judgment came upon
all men to condemnation." [1]

For Adam was the fountainhead of the human race.
He sprang like a crystal-clear spring from the ground,
and was permitted to choose whether he would become
a river running through pleasant and productive green
pastures, or a muddy torrent forever dashing against
rocks and churning between deep, sunless cliffs—cold
and miserable in itself, and unable to bring joy and fruit-
fulness to the surrounding land.

God is not to blame for the tragic snarl in which the
world has so long found itself. The fault lies squarely
with Adam—Adam who was given his choice and who
chose to listen to the lies of the Tempter rather than to
the truth of God! The history of the human race from

[1] *Romans 5:18.*

that day to this has been the story of man's futile effort
to gain back the position that was lost by Adam's fall!

"But this is unfair!" you may say. "Why should we
suffer today, because the first man sinned away back in
the furthest reaches of time? Why hasn't mankind re-
covered during the intervening years? Why should we
go on being punished every day of our lives?"

Let us turn again to the story of the river—the cold,
dark river that runs at the bottom of the deep, dreary
gorge. Why doesn't this river make its way back up to
the warm, pleasant fields that lie above it? Why doesn't
it leave its mournful route and become the happy, bub-
bling stream it was when it burst spontaneously from the
earth?

It doesn't, because it *can't.* It has no power within itself to do other than it has always done. Once it has
plunged down the steep banks into darkness, it cannot
lift itself again to the bright, sunny land above. The
means by which it could be lifted exists, the way is at
hand, but the river does not understand how to make use
of it.

A miracle stands ever ready to bring the river of humanity out of its misery and to place it once more in the
warm valley of peace, but the river doesn't see or heed
it. It feels that it can do nothing but continue on its
tortuous way until it finally loses itself in the sea of
destruction.

The story of the river is the story of man since the time
of Adam, winding, twisting, plunging ever deeper into
the frightening darkness. Though we lift up our voices
and cry out for help, still we deliberately choose—as
Adam did—the wrong way. In our despair we turn against
God and blame Him for our dilemma. We question His
wisdom and judgment. We find fault with His mercy
and love.

We forget that Adam was the head of the human race,
even as in this country our President is the head of our
government. When the President acts, it is really the
American people acting through him. When the Presi-

dent makes a decision, that decision stands as the decision of the entire people.

Adam stands as the federal head of the human race. When he failed, when he succumbed to temptation and fell, the generations yet unborn fell with him, for the Bible states very clearly that the results of Adam's sin shall be visited upon every one of his descendants. We know all too well the bitter truth of those passages in Genesis 3:17-19 which describe the tragedy that Adam's act brought upon us all: "Cursed is the ground for thy sake, in sorrow shalt thou eat of it all the days of thy life; Thorns also and thistles shall it bring forth to thee; and thou shalt eat the herb of the field; In the sweat of thy face shalt thou eat bread, till thou return unto the ground; for out of it wast thou taken: for dust thou art, and unto dust shalt thou return."

And to Eve, God said: "I will greatly multiply thy sorrow and thy conception; in sorrow thou shalt bring forth children; and thy desire shall be to thy husband, and he shall rule over thee." [2]

In other words, because of Adam's original sin, the ground which once bore only beautiful and nourishing plants now produces both good and bad alike. Man, who once had but to walk in the Garden and reach out his hand for food, who had no need for clothing or for shelter, must now toil all the days of his life to provide these necessities for himself and his family. Woman, once the most carefree of creatures, is now burdened with sorrow and pain; and both man and woman are under penalty of spiritual and physical death.

Sin entered the human race through Adam, and the human race has been trying without success to get rid of it ever since. The Bible teaches that God warned Adam before he sinned that if he ate of the tree of knowledge he would surely die. The Bible also tells us that God instructed Adam and Eve to be fruitful and to multiply and to replenish the earth. But although they had been created in the image of God, after the fall Adam

[2] *Genesis 3:16.*

and Eve gave birth to children after their own likeness and image. Consequently Cain and Abel were infected with the death-dealing disease of sin, which they inherited from their parents and which has been passed on to every generation since. We are all sinners by inheritance, and try as we will, we cannot escape our birthright.

We have resorted to every means to win back the position that Adam lost. We have tried through education, through philosophy, through religion, through governments to throw off our yoke of depravity and sin. We have sought to accomplish with our sin-limited minds the things that God intended man to do with the clear vision that can come only from on high. Our motives have been good and some of our attempts have been commendable, but they have all fallen far, far short of the goal. All our knowledge, all our inventions, all our developments and ambitious plans move us ahead only a very little before we drop back again to the point from which we started. For we are still making the same mistake that Adam made—we are still trying to be king in our own right, and with our own power, instead of obeying God's laws.

Before we label God as unjust or unreasonable for permitting sin to envelop the world, let us look at the situation more carefully. God in His infinite compassion sent His Son to show us the way out of our difficulties. He sent His Son to experience the same temptations that were set before Adam and to triumph over them. Satan tempted Jesus, just as he tempted Adam. Satan offered Jesus power and glory if He would forsake God, just as he offered it to Adam through Eve.

The great difference was that Jesus Christ resisted the temptation! When the Devil showed Him all the kingdoms of the world and promised Him all the glory of them if He would but follow Satan instead of God, our blessed Lord said: "Get thee hence, Satan: for it is written, Thou shalt worship the Lord thy God and Him only shalt thou serve." [3] He completely triumphed over the

---

[3] *Matthew 4:10.*

Tempter to reveal to all peoples of all succeeding generations His sinless character.

In our weakness and because of our depraved nature we have proved to be the true sons of Adam and have followed faithfully in his steps. We may curse Adam but we still imitate him!

There is not a single day that we do not face the same test that was set before Adam. There is not a day that we do not have a chance to choose between the Devil's clever promises and God's sure Word. Every day we have the opportunity to move ourselves and others a little closer to that beautiful living Garden that Adam forfeited.

We long for the day to come when disappointment, disease, and death will vanish—but there is no possibility of this dream coming true as long as we are the unregenerate sons of Adam. Something must be done about our sins. In succeeding chapters we will see that God has done something about this basic problem of the human race.

From the beginning of time until the present moment, man's ungodly quest for power, his determination to use his gift of free choice for his own selfish ends, has brought him to the brink of doom. The rubble and ruins of many civilizations lie scattered over the earth's surface—mute testimony to man's inability to build a lasting world without God. New rubble, new misery is being created daily, and yet man plunges on his pernicious way.

God, meanwhile, in His infinite understanding and mercy, has looked on, waiting with a patience and compassion that passes all understanding. He waits to offer individual salvation and peace to the ones who will come to His mercy. The same two paths that God set before Adam still lie before us. We are still free to choose. We are living in a period of grace while God withholds the punishment we so justly deserve.

It is the presence of sin that prevents man from being happy. It is because of sin that man has never been able to obtain the utopia of which he dreams. Every project, every civilization that he builds ultimately fails and falls into oblivion because man's works are all wrought in unrighteousness. The ruins around us at this moment are eloquent witness to the sin that fills the world.

Man seems to have lost sight of the ever-present law of cause and effect that operates on every level of this universe. The effects are plain enough, but the deep-seated, all-prevailing cause seems to be less distinct. Perhaps it is the blight of the modern-day philosophy of "progress" that dims man's vision. Perhaps it is because man is so enamored of this foolish, man-created theory that he clings to the belief that the race is advancing slowly but surely toward ultimate perfection.

Many philosophers will even argue that the present world tragedy is but an incident in the upward march, and they point to other periods in human history when the prospect seemed as bleak and the outcome as hopeless. Philosophers would try to say that the sad conditions through which we are now living are but the birth pangs of a better day! That men are still children groping and stumbling along in the kindergarten of existence, still a long, long way from the mature and sensible beings that they will become centuries hence!

But the Bible makes plain what natural science seems so unwilling to admit—that nature reveals both a Creator and a corrupter. Man blames the Creator for the work of the corrupter. Man forgets that our world is not as God made it; it has been corrupted. God made the world good. Sin despoiled it. God made man innocent, but sin entered and made him vicious. Every manifestation of evil is the result of basic sin—sin that has remained unchanged since the moment it first entered the human race. It may manifest itself in different ways, but fundamentally it is the same sin that causes an African savage to skulk along a jungle trail awaiting his victim with spear in hand, and a well-trained, educated pilot to fly a jet plane over that same jungle ready to bomb an unsuspecting village.

The two men are separated by centuries of culture. One can be said to be much further "progressed" than the other, one has all the advantages of man-made civilization; while the other is still in the "primitive" state—and

yet, are they really so different? Are they not both motivated by fear and distrust of their fellow men? Are
both not selfishly bent on achieving their own goals at
any cost to their brothers? Is a bomb any less savage or
brutal, or more civilized than a naked spear? Can we
hope to find a solution to our problems so long as both
the most "primitive" and the most "progressed" among
us are more eager to kill than to love our neighbors?

All the sorrow, all the bitterness, all the violence, tragedy, heartache and shame of man's history are summed
up in that one little word—*sin*. It isn't a popular word, it
certainly isn't a fashionable word any more—but it's a
terribly true one!

People don't like to be told they are sinners, even as
their parents and grandparents were sinners before them!
Yet the Bible declares, "There is no difference: for all
have sinned, and come short of the glory of God." [4] The
Bible declares that every person on earth is a sinner in
the sight of God; and whenever I hear anyone take exception to so strong a statement, I am reminded of the
story of the church officer who came to talk to the minister one day about sin.

He said to the minister, "Doctor, we of the congregation wish you wouldn't talk quite so much or so plainly
about sin. We feel that if our boys and girls hear you
discuss the subject so much they will all the more easily
become sinners. Why don't you call it a 'mistake' or say
that our young people are often guilty of using 'poor
judgment'—but please don't talk so openly about sin."

The minister walked over and took down a bottle of
poison from a high shelf and showed it to his visitor. The
bottle was plainly marked in big red letters, "Poison! Do
not touch!" "What would you have me do?" asked the
minister. "Do you feel it would be wise for me to remove
this plain label and put on one that read 'Essence of Pep-
permint'? Don't you see that the milder you make the
label, the more dangerous you make the poison?"

Sin—plain old-fashioned sin, the selfsame sin that

_____

[4] *Romans* 3:22-23.

caused Adam's downfall—is what we are all suffering from today, and it will do us far more harm than good to try to dress it up with a fancy, more attractive label. We don't need a new word for it. What we need is to find out what the word we already have means! Because, although sin is certainly prevalent in the world today, there are multitudes of people who are wholly ignorant of its real meaning. It is the misguided, shortsighted view of sin that stands in the way of conversion for many men and women. It is the lack of real understanding of sin that keeps many Christians from living the true life of Christ.

The old spiritual says, "Everybody talkin' 'bout heaven, ain't going there," and the same thing is true of sin. Everybody who talks about sin doesn't have a clear realization of what it means, and it is of supreme importance that we become familiar with the Biblical point of view on the doctrine of sin.

We may try to take a light view of sin and to refer to it as "human weakness." We may try to call it a trifle, but God calls it a tragedy. We would pass it off as an accident, but God declares it is an abomination. Man seeks to excuse himself of sin, but God seeks to convict him of it and to save him from it. Sin is no amusing toy—it is a terror to be shunned! Learn, then, what constitutes sin in the eyes of God!

Dr. Richard Beal gives us five words for sin.

First: sin is *lawlessness*, the transgression of the law of God.[5] God established the boundary line between good and evil, and whenever we overstep that boundary, whenever we are guilty of intrusion into the forbidden area of evil, we are breaking the law. Whenever we fail to live up to the Ten Commandments, whenever we go contrary to the precepts of the Sermon on the Mount, we have transgressed the law of God and are guilty of sin.

James made it plain that we are all guilty when he said: "But every man is tempted, when he is drawn away of his own lust, and enticed. Then when lust hath conceived, it bringeth forth sin: and sin, when it is finished,

[5] 1 John 3:4.

bringeth forth death." [6] It is because we have all broken God's laws, all transgressed His commands that we are all classified as sinners.

Second: the Bible describes sin as *iniquity*. Iniquity is the deviation from right, whether or not the particular act has been expressly forbidden. Iniquity has to do with our inner motivations, the very things that we so often try to keep hidden from the eyes of men and God. They are the wrongs which spring from our own corrupt nature rather than the evil acts which force of circumstances sometimes cause us to commit.

Jesus described this inner corruptness when He said: "From within, out of the heart of men, proceed evil thoughts, adulteries, fornications, murders, thefts, covetousness, wickedness, deceit, lasciviousness, an evil eye, blasphemy, pride, foolishness: All these evil things come from within, and defile the man." [7]

Third: the Bible explains sin as *missing the mark*, falling short of the goal that has been set. God's goal is Christ. The object and end-purpose of all of life is to live up to the life of Christ. He came to show us what it is possible for man to achieve here on earth; and when we fail to follow His example, we miss the mark and fall short of the divine standard.

Fourth: sin is a form of *trespass*. It is the intrusion of self-will into the sphere of divine authority. Sin is not merely a negative thing, it is not just the absence of love for God. Sin is the making of a positive choice, the preference of self instead of God. It is the centering of affection in one's own being instead of reaching out with all your heart to embrace God. Egoism and selfishness are the marks of sin as surely as are theft and murder. Perhaps this is the most subtle and destructive form of sin, for in this form it is so easy to overlook the label on the bottle of poison. Those who cling to themselves, those who center their entire attention on their own beings, those who regard only their own interests and fight to

[6] James 1:14-15.　　　[7] Mark 7:21-23.

protect only their own rights—these are sinners as much
as the drunkard or harlot.

Jesus said: "What shall it profit a man, if he shall gain
the whole world, and lose his own soul?" [8] Translated
into modern terms, could we not say, "What shall it
profit a man to build a vast industrial empire if he is
eaten away by ulcers and can enjoy nothing of life? What
shall it profit a dictator though he conquer a hemisphere
if he must live in constant fear of an avenger's bullet or
an assassin's knife? What shall it profit a parent to bring
up children with harsh domination if he is rejected by
them later and left to a lonely old age?" Verily, the sin
of self is a deadly sin indeed.

Fifth: sin is *unbelief*. Unbelief is a sin because it is an
insult to the truthfulness of God. "He that believeth on
the Son of God hath the witness within himself. He that
believeth not God hath made Him a liar because he believeth not the record that God gave of His Son." [9]

It is unbelief that shuts the door to heaven and opens
it to hell. It is unbelief that rejects the Word of God and
refuses Christ as Savior. It is unbelief that causes men
to turn a deaf ear to the Gospel and to deny the miracles
of Christ.

Sin incurs the penalty of death, and no man has the
ability in himself to save himself from sin's penalty or to
cleanse his own heart of its corruption. Angels and men
cannot atone for sin. It is only in Christ that the remedy
for sin can be found. It is only Christ who can save the
sinner from the fate that surely awaits him. "For the
wages of sin is death." [10] "The soul that sinneth, it shall
die." [11] "None of them can by any means redeem his
brother, nor give to God a ransom for him." [12] "Neither
their silver nor their gold shall be able to deliver them
in the day of the Lord's wrath." [13]

Man's only salvation from sin stands on a lonely, barren, skull-shaped hill; a thief hangs on one cross, a mur-

[8] *Mark 8:36.*   [9] *1 John 5:10.*
[10] *Romans 6:23.*   [11] *Ezekiel 18:4.*
[12] *Psalm 49:7.*   [13] *Zephaniah 1:18.*

derer on another, and between them, a Man with a crown of thorns. Blood flows from His hands and feet, it gushes from His side, it drips above His eyes—while those who stand in comfort before Him sneer and mock Him.

And who is this tortured figure, who is this Man that other men seek to humiliate and kill? He is the Son of God, the Prince of Peace, heaven's own appointed Messenger to the sin-ridden earth. This is He, before whom angels fall down and veil their faces. And yet He hangs bleeding and forsaken upon the cruel tree.

What brought Him to this place of horrors? Who inflicted this hideous torture upon the Man who came to teach us love? *You* did and *I* did, for it was for *your* sin and *my* sin that Jesus was nailed to the cross. In this immortal moment the human race experienced the darkest reaches of sin, it sank to its lowest depths, it touched its foulest limits. No wonder that the sun could not endure and veiled its face!

> *Alas! and did my Savior bleed?*
> *And did my Sov-'reign die?*
> *Would he devote that sacred head*
> *For such a worm as I?*

But sin overreached itself on the cross. The blow that crucified Christ became the blow that opened the gates for man to become free. Sin's masterpiece of shame and hate became God's masterpiece of mercy and forgiveness. Through the death of the Lamb of God upon the cross, sin itself was crucified for those who believe in Christ. His death is the foundation of our hope, the promise of our triumph! Christ bore in His own body on the tree the sins that shackle us. He died for us and rose again. He proved the truth of all God's promises to man; and if you will accept Christ by faith today, you, too, can break the bonds of sin, and stand secure and free in the knowledge that through the love of Christ your soul is cleansed of sin and saved from damnation.

Chapter Five

THE DEVIL

For we wrestle not against flesh and blood, but against principalities, against powers, against the rulers of the darkness of this world, against the spiritual wickedness in high places.

EPHESIANS 6:12.

THERE is a satanic principle involved in all that is happening today. The Bible describes "that old serpent, called the Devil and Satan, which deceiveth the whole world" [1] and we know him to be at work confusing all peoples and all nations. His handiwork is to be seen at every turn.

Let us but take hope that "peace in our time" is drawing closer, and almost overnight misunderstanding, suspicion, and bad faith break out anew and the patient work of months is undone in a moment. For Satan is determined that the dark, joyless river of humanity shall continue on its tormented way until the end of time. He won over Adam in the Garden, and he is convinced that he can claim the souls of Adam's descendants for himself.

There is not a thinking person in the world today who has not wondered many times about the existence of the Devil. That he *does* exist, there is no doubt. We see his power and influence everywhere. The question is not *is* there a Devil, but *how* and *why* did the Devil come to be.

We know from the story of Adam and Eve that the Devil was already present on earth before God made the

[1] *Revelation* 12:9.

45

first man. Evil already existed, else God would not have
made a tree whose fruit gave the awareness of good and
bad. There would have been no necessity for such a tree,
no possibility of it, if evil had not already been present
and man been in need of protection from it.

Here we face the greatest of all mysteries, the most
significant of all secrets, the most unanswerable of all
questions. How could God—who is all-powerful, all-holy
and all-loving—have created evil, or permitted the Devil
to create it? Why did Adam have to be tempted? Why
didn't God strike the Devil dead when he entered the
body of the serpent to whisper evil thoughts to Eve?

The Bible gives us a few hints as to what the answer
may be. But the Bible also makes it very clear that man
is not supposed to know the full answer until God has
allowed the Devil and all his designs to help work out
His own great plan.

Before the fall of Adam, long before Adam even existed, it would appear that God's universe was divided
into spheres of influence, each of which was under the
supervision and control of an angel or heavenly prince,
all of whom were responsible directly to God. Paul tells
us of "thrones, governments, princedoms, and authorities"
in both the visible and the invisible world.[2] The Bible
makes frequent mention of angels and archangels, showing that there was established order among them, some
being more powerful than others.

The Devil must have been just such a powerful, heavenly prince, having the earth assigned to him, perhaps,
as his special province. Known as Lucifer, the "light-
bearer," he must have stood very close to God—so close,
in fact, that ambition entered his heart and he determined to be not God's beloved prince, but to be placed
on an equal footing with God Himself!

It was at that moment that the breach appeared in
the cosmos. It was at that moment that the universe—
which had been all good and all harmonious to God's
will—split, and a portion of it set itself in opposition to

[2] Colossians 1:16; Ephesians 1:21.

God. The Devil defied God and attempted to set up his own authority. He abandoned his own position in the government of God and descended into the lower heavens and cried out that he would be like the Most High God. He had been set by God as the prince of this world; and God has not yet removed him from that position, though the righteous basis for that removal has been laid by the death of Christ. Ever since that moment, the Devil has been contesting God on earth.

As a mighty prince, with hosts of angels at his command, he has set up his kingdom on earth. His power and position here are the very reasons that the Scriptures came to be written. Had Satan not defied God and attempted to rival His power and authority, the story of Adam in the Garden would have been very different. Had Satan not set himself in opposition to God, there would have been no need to give mankind the Ten Commandments, there would have been no need for God to send His Son to the cross.

Jesus and His apostles were well aware of the Devil. Matthew records an actual conversation between Jesus and the Devil.[3] The Devil was very real to the Pharisees —so real, in fact, that they accused Jesus of being the Devil himself! [4] There was no doubt in Jesus' mind of the existence of the Devil, nor of the power that he wields here on earth.

The Devil's strength is clearly demonstrated in the passage from Jude 9 which relates: "Yet Michael the archangel, when contending with the devil he disputed about the body of Moses, durst not bring against him a railing accusation, but said, The Lord rebuke thee."

Modern confusion about the personality of the Devil has resulted in large measure from the caricatures of him which became popular during the Middle Ages. To allay their fear of the Devil, people tried to laugh at him, and pictured him as a foolish, grotesque creature with horns and a long tail. They put a pitchfork in his hand, and a feeble-minded leer on his face, and then said to them-

[3] *Matthew 4:1-10.*   [4] *Matthew 12:24.*

selves, "Who's afraid of a ridiculous figure like this?"

The truth is that the Devil is a creature of vastly superior intelligence, a mighty and gifted spirit of infinite resourcefulness. We forget that the Devil was perhaps the greatest and most exalted of all God's angels. He was a sublime figure, who decided to use his divine endowments for his own aims instead of God's. His reasoning is brilliant, his plans ingenious, his logic well-nigh irrefutable. God's mighty adversary is no bungling creature with horns and tail—he is a prince of lofty stature, of unlimited craft and cunning, able to take advantage of every opportunity that presents itself, able to turn every situation to his own advantage.

The Devil is quite capable of bringing forth the false prophet of which the Bible warns. Upon the wreckage of disbelief and faltering faith the Devil will set his masterpiece, the counterfeit king. He will create a religion without a Redeemer. He will build a church without a Christ. He will call for worship without the Word of God.

The Apostle Paul predicted this when he said: "But I fear, lest by any means, as the serpent beguiled Eve through his subtlety, so your minds should be corrupted from the simplicity that is Christ. For if he that cometh preacheth another Jesus, whom we have not preached, or if ye receive another spirit, which ye have not received, or another gospel, which ye have not accepted, ye might well bear with him ... For such are false apostles, deceitful workers, transforming themselves into the apostles of Christ." [5]

We know that the anti-Christ will appear and try to ensnare the minds and hearts of men. The time draws close, the stage is set—confusion, panic, and fear are abroad. The signs of the false prophet are everywhere at hand, and many may be the living witnesses of the awesome moment when the final act of this age-old drama begins. It may well come in our time, for the tempo is speeding up, events move more swiftly, and on every side

[5] 2 Corinthians 11:3-4,13.

we see men and women consciously or unconsciously choosing up sides—aligning themselves with the Devil or with God.

It will be a battle to the death, in the truest meaning of that word—a battle that will give no quarter, that will make no allowances or exceptions. The human phase of this battle started in the Garden of Eden when the Devil seduced mankind from God, making it possible for there to be billions of warring wills, every man turning to his own way. "All we like sheep have gone astray; we have turned every one to his own way; and the LORD hath laid on Him the iniquity of us all." [6] It will continue until the end of time, until one or the other of these two mighty forces—the force of good or evil—triumphs and places the True King or the false king on the throne.

At this moment in history, two mighty trinities stand face to face: the Trinity of God (the Father, Son, and Holy Ghost) and the false trinity that Satan would have us worship in its place. The trinity of evil (the Devil, anti-Christ, and false prophet) is described in the Book of Revelation: "And I saw three unclean spirits like frogs come out of the dragon, and out of the mouth of the beast, and out of the mouth of the false prophet." [7]

Never for a second of your waking or sleeping life are you without these two powerful forces, never is there a moment when you cannot deliberately choose to go with one or the other. Always the Devil is standing at your side tempting, coaxing, threatening, cajoling. And always on your other side stands Jesus, the all-loving, the all-forgiving, waiting for you to turn to Him and ask His aid, waiting to give you supernatural power to resist the evil one.

In moments of your greatest fear and anxiety, in moments when you feel yourself helpless in the grip of events you cannot control, when despair and disappointment overwhelm you—in these moments many times it is the Devil who is trying to catch you at your weakest

[6] *Isaiah 53:6.*   [7] *Revelation 16:13.*

point and push you further along the path that Adam
took.

In these perilous moments remember that Christ has
not deserted you. He has not left you defenseless. As
He triumphed over Satan in His hour of temptation and
trial, so He has promised that you, too, can have daily
victory over the Tempter. Remember: "For this purpose
the Son of God was manifested, that He might *make inoperative* the works of the devil." [8]

The same Book that tells us over and over again of
God's love, warns us constantly of the Devil that would
come between us and God, the Devil who is ever waiting
to ensnare men's souls. "Be sober, be vigilant; because
your adversary the devil, as a roaring lion, walketh about,
seeking whom he may devour." [9] The Bible describes
a personal Devil who controls a host of demon spirits
that attempt to dominate and control all human activity,
"The prince of the power of the air, the spirit that now
worketh in the children of disobedience." [10]

Don't doubt for a moment the existence of the Devil!
He is very personal and he is very real! And he is extremely clever! Look again at the front page of today's
newspaper if you have any question about the personality
of the Devil. Switch on your local radio or television
news commentator if you feel you need concrete evidence!

Would sane, thinking men and women behave in this
way if they were not in the grip of evil? Could hearts
filled only with God's love and God's goodness conceive
and carry out the acts of violence and malice that are
reported to us every day? Could men of education, intelligence, and honest intent gather around a world conference table and fail so completely to understand each
other's needs and goals if their thinking was not being
deliberately clouded and corrupted?

Whenever I hear an "enlightened" person of our time
take issue with the plausibility of a personal, individual-

[8] *1 John 3:8.*   [9] *1 Peter 5:8.*
[10] *Ephesians 2:2.*

ized Devil in command of a host of evil spirits, I am reminded of this poem by Alfred J. Hough:

Men don't believe in the Devil now, as their fathers
*   used to do;*
They've forced the door of the broadest creed to let
*   his majesty through.*
There isn't a print of his cloven foot or fiery dart
*   from his brow*
To be found on earth or air today, for the world has
*   voted it so.*

Who dogs the steps of the toiling saint and digs the
*   pits for his feet?*
Who sows the tares in the fields of time whenever
*   God sows the wheat?*
The Devil is voted not to be, and of course, the thing
*   is true;*
But who is doing the kind of work that the Devil
*   alone can do?*

We are told that he doesn't go about as a
*   roaring lion now;*
But whom shall we hold responsible for the
*   everlasting row*
To be heard in home, in church and state, to
*   the earth's remotest bound,*
If the Devil by unanimous vote is
*   nowhere to be found?*

Won't someone step to the front forthwith
*   and make their bow and show*
How the frauds and crimes of a single day spring up?
*   We want to know!*
The Devil was fairly voted out, and of course,
*   the Devil's gone;*
But simple people would like to know who carries
*   the business on?*

Who, indeed, is responsible for the infamy, terror, and

agony that we see all around us? How can we account
for the sufferings that we all experience if evil is not a
potent force? Modern education has, in truth, impeded
our minds if, because of allegedly scientific findings, we
have lost our belief in the supernatural powers of Satan.

George Galloway summed up this dubious contribution
of current education when he said: "The theory that
there is in the universe a power or principle, personal or
otherwise, in eternal opposition to God is generally dis-
carded by the modern mind."

The modern mind may discard it, but that doesn't
cause the evil principle itself to disappear!

The great Methodist preacher, Dr. Clovis Chappell,
writes, in his *Sermons from the Parables:* "It seems that
Jesus, along with the saints of the New Testament, believed that there was an evil personality known as the
Devil . . . Our day has thrown this doctrine aside." But
he is careful to add: "If we can no longer account for
the presence of evil by charging it up to the Devil, we
do not for this reason do away with the fact of evil. Sin
is a grim fact, explain it however we may."

Sin is certainly a grim fact! It stands like a titanic force,
contesting all the good that men may try to accomplish.
It stands like a dark shadow, ever ready to blot out whatever light may reach us from on high. We all know this.
We all see it. We all are conscious of it in every move
we make. Call it what we may, we know of its very real
existence. "For we wrestle not against flesh and blood,
but against principalities, against the powers, against the
rulers of the darkness of this world, against spiritual
wickedness in high places." [11]

How do those who deny the Devil and his minions account for the speed with which evil spreads? How do
they explain the endless stumbling blocks that are placed
in the path of the righteous? How can they reason away
the fact that destruction and disaster are but the work of
seconds, while construction and rehabilitation are often
agonizingly slow?

[11] *Ephesians 6:12.*

Breathe a lie into the air, let loose a slanderous tongue —and the words are carried as by magic to the farthest corners. Speak a truth, perform a generous and honest act—and unseen powers will be at work at once to try to hide this tiny ray of light and hope.

No one deliberately builds churches to the Devil, no one constructs pulpits to preach his word. Yet his word is everywhere, and all too often his word is translated into desperate deeds. If no unseen power is at work corrupting men's hearts and distorting men's thoughts, how can you explain humanity's eagerness to listen to the base and vulgar and vile, while it turns a deaf ear to the good and clean and pure?

Would one single person among us ever pass up a piece of ripe delicious fruit to select a rotten piece that was crawling with worms and reeking with decay, if we were not driven to this dreadful choice by a great and sinister power? Yet that is exactly what we all do over and over again. We constantly pass up the rich and beautiful and ennobling experiences and seek out the tawdry, the cheap, and the degrading. These are the works of the Devil, and they flourish on every side!

What we see happening here on earth is but a reflection of the far vaster struggles between good and evil in the unseen realm. We like to think that our planet is the center of the universe, and we attach too much importance to earthly events. Our foolish pride is such that we can only recognize and take into account that which is apparent to our human eyes. But a struggle of infinitely greater magnitude is being waged in the world we cannot see!

The wise men of old knew this. They were aware that there is much that the human eye fails to discern and much to which the human ear is deaf. Modern man likes to feel that he "created" radio and television, that he made it possible to send audible sounds and visible images through space. The truth is, of course, that these waves, unknown to man, have always existed, and that far greater wonders are in space, of which man may never gain the slightest knowledge. That these wonders were there, the ancient prophets knew—but even they had but a suggestion of their magnitude, even they could catch but the faintest echoes of the mighty battle of the spheres.

One of the many prices Adam paid for listening to the Devil was to lose the vision of spiritual dimensions. He lost for himself and all of humanity the capacity for seeing and hearing and understanding anything that was not basely material. Adam closed himself off from the eternal wonders and splendors of the unseen world. He lost the power of true prophecy, the ability to look ahead, and by so doing to better understand and perform the work of the present. He lost his sense of continuity, of oneness with the universe and with all living things. He separated himself from God and became an alien being in God's world.

When Adam did this he became somewhat like a defective television receiver that is capable of tuning in only one channel instead of many—and that one channel is distorted and confused!

If we find a television image to be blurred and out of focus, we do not blame the transmitting station for it. When we cannot get the program that we want, or when the picture on the screen becomes indistinct, we do not damn the scientists who devised the tubes that make television possible. We recognize that the fault lies with the particular set we are using. We do not say that all of television is a miserable failure because our antenna may be improperly installed, or we live in a neighborhood where TV reception is poor!

But let tragedy or sickness come to us, let us suffer the consequences of our own sins, and we immediately blame God for it! We are patient and understanding with our television sets when they do not give us what we want, but we are quick to rail against God and His universe when we get a distorted picture of it.

Let someone get the business promotion we wanted, let someone we consider less deserving succeed where we have failed, and we cry out against God's injustice. We demand to know why God permits such inequalities!

We lose sight of the fact that God, like a great master television station, is sending out a perfect image of love and righteousness all the time, and that the faulty reception lies with us!

It is the evil and distortion within ourselves that keeps us from seeing and experiencing God's perfect world. It is our own sin that blurs the image, that keeps us from being God's pure children instead of the children of evil. Paul spoke for all of us when he said: "For the good that I would I do not, but the evil which I would not, that I do." [12] Paul recognized the dreaded enemy, the powerful foe of all mankind, and cried out, "O wretched man that I am! who shall deliver me from the body of this death? I thank God through Jesus Christ our Lord. So then with the mind I myself serve the law of God; but with the flesh the law of sin." [13]

Two overwhelming adversaries were clearly apparent to Paul, and he was acutely aware of being torn between their mighty magnetisms. The power of good was pulling his mind and heart toward God, while the power of evil was trying to drag his body down into death and destruction.

You are caught between these same two forces: life and death! Choose God's way, and there is life. Choose Satan's way, and it is death!

[12] *Romans 7:19.*   [13] *Romans 7:24-25.*

Chapter Six

AFTER DEATH—WHAT?

There is but a step between me and death.
1 SAMUEL 20:3.

IT HAS been said that all of life is but a preparation for death.

The Psalmist said: "What man is he that liveth, and shall not see death?" [1]

This is supposed to be a freethinking age of radical experiment. We have sought to change the world and the laws which govern it through knowledge, science, invention, discovery, philosophy, and materialistic thinking. We have tried to enthrone the false gods of money, fame, and human intelligence; but however we try, the end is always the same: "It is appointed unto men once to die." [2]

In the midst of life, we see death on every hand. The wail of the ambulance, the illuminated mortuary signs, the graveyards we so frequently pass, and the sight of a hearse threading its way through traffic, all remind us that the Grim Reaper may call for us at any moment. None of us can be sure when that exact moment will be, but we are well aware that it may come at any time.

Dr. John S. Wimbish has put it aptly: "Our lives hang by such brittle threads. The grave darkly gapes at our feet every step of life's journey. Death is the universal adversary. Even kings must succumb to the Grim Reap-

[1] *Psalm 89:48.*   [2] *Hebrews 9:27.*

er's scythe. Scientist and surgeon battle valiantly to keep the monster from palace doors, but the shrouded Monarch of Terrors stealthily steals past the guards and down the corridors and, in the royal bedchambers, envelops the mighty potentate in his somber cloak."

Each year some forty thousand Americans step into their automobiles little realizing this is to be their last ride. In spite of all the increased safety measures, another thirty thousand persons are killed in accidents at home, when all thought of death is far from their minds. For death stalks mankind relentlessly, and although medical science and safety engineers wage a constant war against it, in the end, death is always the victor.

Because of this long-fought scientific battle, we now have the advantage of a few years more of life, but death is still standing at the end of the road, and the life span of the average person does not far exceed the Biblical three score years and ten.

Heart diseases still cut down far too many of our citizens in the prime of life. Cancer still presses its pain into the bodies of thousands. Tuberculosis, blood diseases, polio, and pneumonia take their toll, although medical research has greatly decreased their annual number. But however optimistic the statistical surveys, however much our life span has been increased since 1900, whatever the figures may show on murder, suicide, and other forms of violent death, the inevitable fact of death remains unchanged—it is still our ultimate experience on earth!

From the moment a child is born, the fight against death begins. The mother devotes years of attention to the protection of the life of her child. She watches the food, the clothes, the environment, the medical checkups and inoculations, but in spite of her loving care, the child has already begun to die.

Before many years the tangible signs of weakness will be obvious. The dentist will check the decay of our teeth. Glasses will be needed to help improve our fading vision. Skin will wrinkle and sag as time passes, and our shoulders will droop and our step become slower and less sure. The brittleness of our bones will increase as our energy lessens, and almost without realizing it we have begun to move closer to death.

Health insurance and hospitalization will be used to help us cushion the blow. Life insurance will be purchased to cover our final expenses and obligations, and we shall suddenly see our whole life as a great and never-ending battle with death. We shall see that we are all running a race in which the most we can hope for is a little more time, and outwit our opponent as we may, in the end we know that death will always win!

What a mysterious thing is this enemy of ours—as mysterious as life itself. For the life that we see so plentifully around us in plants and animals, as well as in human beings, cannot be reproduced by us, or even explained. Death is also without explanation, although we are as aware of its presence as we are of life. How little we like to talk about it, however, or consider its importance! When life comes, and a child is born, we rejoice. When life goes, and a man dies, we try to dismiss the thought as quickly as possible.

Does it not seem strange, though, since so much of our energy is directed toward bringing life into the world, that we should turn our backs so resolutely upon the equally important fact of the departure of this same life from the earth?

Today there are something like two billion people living on this planet. Almost all of them will be dead in a hundred years. Their bodies will be without feeling. But what about their souls—the essential and eternal part of life? Here is the mystery. What is missing when a man dies? Where does that missing thing go?

Two years ago a newspaper columnist died in Denver, Colorado. The mourners listened to his recorded voice at the funeral when he said, "This is my funeral. I am an atheist and have been for many years. I have the utmost contempt for theological nonsense. Clergymen are moral cowards. Miracles are the product of the imagination. If any four reporters were sent to an execution and got their facts as twisted as the apostles in the Bible report, they would be fired forthwith. I want no religious songs. This is going to be a perfectly rational funeral."

Every age has produced men who in their hatred of God have attempted to heap ridicule and abuse upon the church, the Scripture, and Jesus Christ. Without presenting evidence they cry out against the voice of God. History testifies of the George Bernard Shaws, the Robert Ingersolls, and many other philosophers who strove, by argument, to destroy the fear of death.

Listen to the anthropologist tell of death in the jungle. There is no "theological nonsense" there, for they have not heard of Jesus Christ. What of death there? In some tribes the old are turned into the bush so that the wild animals might attack them and death need not be faced by the young. In another tribe the clothes are stripped off and the bodies of the mourners painted with white. Hour after hour the moans and screams of the women tell the world that a soul is about to leave a body. Death outside of Christian influence is filled with horror and despair.

Compare this to the death of the Christian. When Christ came He gave a new approach to death. Man had always looked upon death as an enemy, but Jesus said that He had conquered death and taken the very sting out of death. Jesus Christ was the Master Realist when He urged men to prepare for death, which was certain to come. Do not worry, said the Lord Jesus, about the death of the body, but rather concern yourself with the eternal death of the soul.

The Bible indicates that there are actually two deaths: one is *physical death* and the other is *eternal death*. Jesus warned that we are to fear the *second death* far more than the *first death*. He described the *second death* as hell, which is eternal separation from God. He indicated that the death of your body is nothing compared to the conscious everlasting banishment of a soul from God.

The last statements of dying men provide an excellent study for those who are looking for realism in the face of death. Dr. Wilbur Smith in his outstanding book *Therefore, Stand* provides several stories of the closing hours of some famous non-Christians.

How different is the story of the Christian who has confessed his sin and by faith received Jesus Christ as his personal Savior.

For many years Dr. Effie Jane Wheeler taught English and literature where I attended college. Dr. Wheeler was noted for her piety as well as for her knowledge of the subjects she taught. In May of 1949, on Memorial Day, Dr. Wheeler wrote the following letter to Dr. Edman, president of the college, her colleagues, and former students:

"I greatly appreciate the moment in chapel that may be given to reading this, for before you leave for the summer I should like to have you know the truth about me as I learned it myself only last Friday. My doctor at last has given what has been his real diagnosis of my illness for weeks—an inoperable case of cancer. Now if he had been a Christian he wouldn't have been so dilatory or shaken, for he would have known, as you and I do, that life or death is equally welcome when we live in the will and presence of the Lord. If the Lord has chosen me to go to Him soon, I go gladly. Please do not give a moment's grief for me. I do not say a cold goodbye but rather a warm *Auf Wiedersehen* till I see you again—in the blessed land where I may be allowed to draw aside a curtain when you enter. With a heart full of love for every individual of you. [Signed] Effie Jane Wheeler."

Just two weeks after writing this letter, Dr. Wheeler entered the presence of her Lord and Master, who had kept His promise to take the sting out of death.

The Bible teaches that you are an immortal soul. Your soul is eternal and will live forever. In other words, the real you—the part of you that thinks, feels, dreams, aspires; the ego, the personality—will never die. The Bible teaches that your soul will live forever in one of two places—heaven or hell. If you are not a Christian and you have never been born again, then the Bible teaches your soul goes immediately to a place Jesus called Hades, where you will await the judgment of God.

I am conscious of the fact that the subject of hell is not a very pleasant one. It is very unpopular, controversial, and misunderstood. In my campaigns across the country, however, I usually devote one evening to the discussion of this subject. Following my discussion many letters to the editors of newspapers appear for days as people argue the pros and cons, for the Bible has almost as much to say about this subject as any other. In student discussions on many campuses of America I am continually asked the question, "What about hell? Is there fire in hell?" and similar questions. As a minister I must deal with it. I cannot ignore it, even though it makes people uncomfortable and anxious. I grant that it is the hardest of all teachings of Christianity to receive.

There are those who teach that everybody eventually will be saved, that God is a God of love and He will never send anyone to hell. They believe that the words *eternal* or *everlasting* do not actually mean forever. However, the same word which speaks of eternal banishment from God is also used for the eternity of heaven. Someone has said that "fairness demands that we make the joy of the righteous and the punishment of the wicked both qualify, as they are the same Greek word and of the same duration."

There are others who teach that after death those who have refused to receive God's plan of redemption are annihilated, they cease to exist. In searching the Bible from cover to cover I cannot find one shred of evidence to support this view. The Bible teaches that whether we are saved or lost, there is conscious and everlasting existence of the soul and personality.

There are others who teach that after death there is still a possibility of salvation, that God will offer a second chance. If this is true, the Bible gives no hint of it because the Bible is continually warning that "now is the accepted time; behold, now is the day of salvation." [3]

Scores of passages of Scripture could be quoted to support the fact that the Bible does teach there is hell for every man who willingly and knowingly rejects Christ as Lord and Savior:

[3] *2 Corinthians 6:2.*

"I am tormented in this flame." [4]

"Whosoever shall say, Thou fool, shall be in danger of hell fire." [5]

"The Son of Man shall send forth His angels, and they shall gather out of His kingdom all things that offend, and them which do iniquity; and shall cast them into a furnace of fire: there shall be wailing and gnashing of teeth." [6]

"So shall it be at the end of the world: the angels shall come forth, and sever the wicked from among the just, and shall cast them into the furnace of fire: there shall be wailing and gnashing of teeth." [7]

"Then shall He say also unto them on the left hand, Depart from me, ye cursed, into everlasting fire, prepared for the devil and his angels." [8]

"But He will burn up the chaff with unquenchable fire." [9]

"In flaming fire taking vengeance on them that know not God, and that obey not the gospel of our Lord Jesus Christ: Who shall be punished with everlasting destruction from the presence of the Lord, and from the glory of His power." [10]

"The same shall drink of the wine of the wrath of God, which is poured out without mixture into the cup of His indignation; and he shall be tormented with fire and brimstone in the presence of the holy angels, and in the presence of the Lamb: and the smoke of their torment ascendeth up for ever and ever: and they have no rest day nor night." [11]

"And death and hell were cast into the lake of fire. This is the second death. And whosoever was not found written in the Book of Life was cast into the lake of fire." [12]

"But the fearful, and unbelieving, and the abominable, and murderers, and whoremongers, and sorcerers, and

[4] *Luke 16:24.*
[5] *Matthew 5:22.*
[6] *Matthew 13:41-42.*
[7] *Matthew 13:49-50.*
[8] *Matthew 25:41.*
[9] *Matthew 3:12.*
[10] *2 Thessalonians 1:8-9.*
[11] *Revelation 14:10-11.*
[12] *Revelation 20:14-15.*

idolators, and all liars, shall have their part in the lake which burneth with fire and brimstone: which is the second death." [13]

But I hear someone say, "I don't believe in hell. My religion is the Sermon on the Mount."

Well, let's listen to a passage from the Sermon on the Mount: "And if thy right eye offend thee, pluck it out, and cast it from thee: for it is profitable for thee that one of thy members should perish, and not that thy whole body should be cast into hell. And if thy right hand offend thee, cut it off, and cast it from thee: for it is profitable for thee that one of thy members should perish, and not that thy whole body should be cast into hell." [14]

Here we have the distinct teaching of Jesus that there is a hell. In fact, Jesus told stories and gave illustrations on the subject and warned men time after time about the folly of living a sinful and hypocritical life here on earth.

There is no doubt that wicked men suffer a certain hell here on earth. The Bible says, "Be sure your sin will find you out." [15] Again the Bible says, "Whatsoever a man soweth, that shall he also reap." [16] However, there is evidence all around us to show that some wicked men seem to prosper and the righteous suffer for their righteousness. The Bible teaches that there is going to be a time of equalization when justice shall be done.

Will a loving God send a man to hell? The answer is— yes! But He does not send him willingly. Man condemns himself by his refusal of God's way of salvation. In love and mercy, God is offering to men and women a way of escape, a way of salvation, a hope and anticipation of better things. Man in his blindness, stupidity, stubbornness, egotism, and love of sinful pleasure refuses God's simple method of escaping the pangs of eternal banishment.

Suppose you were sick and called a doctor, who came and gave you a prescription. But after thinking it over you decided to ignore his advice and to refuse the medi-

[13] *Revelation 21:8.* [14] *Matthew 5:29-30.*
[15] *Numbers 32:23.* [16] *Galations 6:7.*

cine. When he returned a few days later he might have found your condition much worse. Could you blame the doctor, could you hold him responsible? He gave you the prescription. He prescribed the remedy. But you refused it!

Just so, God prescribes the remedy for the ills of the human race. That remedy is personal faith and commitment to Jesus Christ. The remedy is to be born again, as we will discuss in another chapter. If we deliberately refuse it, then we must suffer the consequences; and we cannot blame God. Is it God's fault because we refuse the remedy?

There are others who ask, "What is the nature of hell?" There are four words that have been translated in our Bible as "hell." One word is *Sheol*, which is translated thirty-one times as "hell" in the Old Testament. It means an "unseen state." The words of *sorrow, pain,* and *destruction* are used in connection with it.

The second word is *Hades,* which is translated from the Greek and used ten times in the New Testament. It means the same as *Sheol* in the Old Testament. Judgment and suffering are always connected with it.

The third word is *Tartarus,* used only once in 2 Peter 2:4, where it says that disobedient angels are cast into Tartarus. It indicates a place of judgment, such as a prison, dungeon, where there is intense darkness.

The fourth word is *Gehenna,* used eleven times, and translated as "hell" in the New Testament. It is the illustration that Jesus used of the Valley of Hinnon, a place outside Jerusalem where rubbish and debris were burned continually.

Others ask, "Does the Bible teach literal fire in hell?" There is no doubt that the Bible many times uses the word *fire* figuratively. However, God does have a fire that burns and yet does not consume.

When Moses saw the bush of fire, he was amazed to find that the bush was not consumed. The three Hebrew children were put in a fiery furnace, but they were not consumed; in fact, not a hair of their heads was singed.

On the other hand, the Bible talks about our tongues'

being "set on fire of hell" [17] every time we speak evil about our neighbors. That does not mean that literal combustion takes place every time we say something against our neighbors. But whether it be literal or figurative does not affect its reality. If there is no fire then God is using symbolic language to indicate something that could be far worse.

Essentially, hell is separation from God. It is the second death, which is described as the eternal conscious banishment from the presence of all that is light, joyous, good, righteous, and happy. The Bible has many fearful descriptions concerning this awful condition in which the soul will find itself one minute after death.

It is strange that men will prepare for everything except death. We prepare for education. We prepare for business. We prepare for our careers. We prepare for marriage. We prepare for old age. We prepare for everything except the moment we are to die. And yet the Bible says it is appointed unto all of us once to die.

Death is an occurrence that to each man seems unnatural when related to himself, but natural when related to others. Death reduces all men to the same rank. It strips the rich of his millions and the poor man of his rags. It cools avarice and stills the fires of passion. All would like to ignore death, and yet all must face it—the prince and the peasant, the fool and the philosopher, the murderer and the saint alike. Death knows no age limits, no partiality. It is a thing that all men fear.

Toward the end of his life, Daniel Webster related how once he attended a church service in a quiet country village. The clergyman was a simplehearted, pious old man. After the opening exercises he arose and pronounced his text, and then with the utmost simplicity and earnestness said, "My friends, we can die but once."

Daniel Webster, commenting on this sermon, later said, "Frigid and weak as these words might seem, at once they were to me among the most impressive and awakening I ever heard."

[17] James 3:6.

It is easy to think of others having to keep this appointment with death, but difficult for us to remember that we, too, must keep this same appointment. When we see soldiers going to the front or read of a condemned prisoner or visit a mortally stricken friend, we are conscious of a certain solemnity which gathers about such persons. Death is appointed for all, and the question of its occurrence is merely a matter of time. Other appointments in life—the appointment of business or of pleasure—we can neglect or break and take the consequence, but here is an appointment that no man can ignore, no man can break. He can meet it only *once*, but meet it he must!

If physical death were the only consequence of a life lived apart from God, we would not have so much to fear, but the Bible warns that there is the second death, which is the eternal banishment from God.

However, there is a brighter side. As the Bible pronounces hell for the sinner, it also promises heaven for the saint. The subject of heaven is much easier to accept than the subject of hell. And yet the Bible teaches both.

If you are moving to a new home, you want to know all about the community to which you are going. If you are transferring to another city, you want to know all about the city—its railroads, industries, parks, lakes, schools, et cetera. And since we are going to spend eternity someplace, we ought to know something about it. The information concerning heaven is found in the Bible. It is right that we should think about it and talk about it. In talking about heaven, earth grows shabby by comparison. Our sorrows and problems here seem so much less when we have keen anticipation of the future. In a certain sense the Christian has heaven here on earth. He has peace of soul, peace of conscience, and peace with God. In the midst of troubles and difficulties he can smile. He has a spring in his step, a joy in his soul, a smile on his face.

But the Bible also promises the Christian a heaven in the life hereafter. Someone asked John Quincy Adams at the age of ninety-four how he felt one morning. He said, "Quite well. Quite well. But the house I live in is not so good." Even though the house we live in may be sick and weak, yet we can actually feel strong and sure if we are Christians. Jesus taught there is a heaven.

There are a number of passages that could be quoted, but the most descriptive is found in John 14:2: "In my Father's house are many rooms. If it were not so, I would have told you. I go to prepare a place for you. And if I go and prepare a place for you, I will come again and receive you unto myself that where I am there ye may be also." Paul was so certain of heaven that he could say, "We are confident, I say, and willing rather to be absent from the body and to be present with the Lord." [18]

How different is the anticipation of the Christian and that of the agnostic Bob Ingersoll, who said at the grave of his brother, "Life is a narrow veil between the cold and barren peaks of two eternities. We strive in vain to look beyond the heights. We cry aloud and the only answer is the echo of our wailing cry."

The Apostle Paul said time after time, "We know," "We are confident," "We are always confident." The Bible says that Abraham "looked for a city which hath foundations, whose builder and maker is God."

Many people say, "Do you believe that heaven is a literal place?" Yes! Jesus said, "I go to prepare *a place* for you." The Bible teaches that Enoch and Elijah ascended in a literal body to a literal place that is just as real as Los Angeles, London, or Algiers!

Many people have asked, "Where is heaven?" We are not told in the Scripture where heaven is. Some students have tried to take some Scriptures and put them together and say that heaven is in the north. They quote Psalm 48:2 that says, "Beautiful for situation, the joy of the whole earth, is mount Zion, on the sides of the north, the city of the great King." It is interesting to note that God gave Moses instructions to pour the blood of the sacrifice on the north side of the altar toward God. The magnetic needle points north. Perhaps the Celestial City

[18] *2 Corinthians* 5:8.

is in the north. We do not know. But no matter where heaven is, it will be where Christ is.

The Bible teaches that this country will be a place of beauty. It is described in the Bible as "a building of God"—"a city"—"a better country"—"an inheritance"—"a glory."

You may ask, "Will we know each other in heaven?" The Bible indicates in a number of places that it will be a time of grand reunion with those who have gone on before.

Others say, "Do you believe that children will be saved?" Yes. The Bible indicates that God does not hold a child accountable for his or her sins until he reaches the age of accountability. There seems to be plenty of indication that the atonement covers their sin until they reach an age at which they are responsible for their own right and wrong actions.

The Bible also indicates that heaven will be a place of great understanding and knowledge of things that we never learned down here.

Sir Isaac Newton, when an old man, said to one who praised his wisdom, "I am as a child on the seashore picking up a pebble here and a shell there, but the great ocean of truth still lies before me."

And Thomas Edison once said, "I do not know one millionth part of one per cent about anything."

Many of the mysteries of God, the heartaches, trials, disappointments, tragedies, and the silence of God in the midst of suffering will be revealed there.

Many people ask, "Well, what will we do in heaven? Just sit down and enjoy the luxuries of life?" No. The Bible indicates that we will serve God. There will be work to do for God. We will spend much time praising Him. The Bible says, "And there shall be no more curse; but the throne of God and of the Lamb shall be in it; and His servants shall serve Him." [19]

It will be a time of joy, service, laughter, singing, and praise to God.

[19] *Revelation* 22:3.

Now the Bible teaches to be absent from the body is to be present with the Lord. The moment a Christian dies, he goes immediately into the presence of Christ. There his soul awaits the resurrection, when the soul and body will be rejoined.

Many people ask, "How can the bodies that have decayed and been cremated be raised?" Scientists have already proved that no chemicals disappear from the earth. The God who made the body in the first place can bring all the original chemicals back together again, and the body will be raised to join the soul. But the new body that we will have will be a glorious body like unto the body of Christ. It will be an eternal body. It will never know tears, heartache, tragedy, disease, suffering, or death.

Here we have a picture of two eternal worlds floating out into space. Every son of Adam will be on one or the other. There is a great deal of mystery surrounding both of them, but there are enough hints and implications in the Bible to give us light that one will be a world of tragedy and suffering and the other will be one of light and glory.

We have now seen the problems of the human race. Superficially, they are complex; basically, they are simple. We have seen that they could probably be summed up in one word—*sin*. We have seen that man's future is hopeless without God. But just to analyze our problems and have an intellectual understanding of God's plan is not enough. If God is to aid man, then man must meet certain conditions. In the next few chapters we will survey these conditions.

PART TWO: THE SOLUTION

Chapter Seven

WHY JESUS CAME

For I delivered unto you first of all that which I also received, how that Christ died for our sins according to the scriptures; And that he was buried, and that he rose again the third day according to the scriptures.
1 CORINTHIANS 15:3-4.

WE HAVE seen that the most terrible, the most devastating fact of the universe is sin. The cause of all trouble, the root of all sorrow, the dread of every man lies in this one small word—*sin*. It has reversed the nature of man. It has destroyed the inner harmony of man's life. It has robbed him of his nobility. It has caused man to be caught in the Devil's trap.

All mental disorders, all sicknesses, all destruction, all wars find their root in sin. It causes madness in the brain, and poison in the heart. It is described in the Bible as a dread and prostrating disease that demands a radical cure. It is a tornado on the loose. It is a volcano gone wild. It is a madman broken loose from the asylum. It is a gangster on the prowl. It is a roaring lion seeking its prey. It is a streak of lightning heading toward the earth. It is a guillotine cutting off the head. It is a deadly cancer eating its way into the souls of men. It is a raging torrent that sweeps everything before it.

"Because of sin every stream with human crime is stained, every breeze is morally corrupted, every day's light is blackened, every life's cup tainted with the bitter, every life's roadway made dangerous with pitfalls, every life's voyage made perilous with treacherous shoals. Sin—destructive of all happiness, darkening understanding,

73

searing conscience, withering everything, causing all tears
of sorrow and all pangs of agony, promising velvet and
giving a shroud, promising liberty and giving bondage,
promising nectar and giving gall, promising silk and giving the shirt of sackcloth."

For ages men were lost in spiritual darkness, blinded
by the disease of sin, made to grope—searching, questing,
seeking some way out. Man needed someone who could
lead him out of the mental confusion and moral laby-
rinth, someone who could redeem him from the Devil's
prison, someone who could unlock the prison doors. Men
with hungry hearts, thirsty minds, and broken spirits
stood hopelessly with searching eyes and listening ears.
Meanwhile the Devil gloated over his mighty victory in
the Garden of Eden.

From the primitive man in the jungle through the
mighty civilizations of Egypt, Greece, and Rome, bewil-
dered men were all asking the same question, "How can
I get out? How can I be better? What can I do? Which
way can I turn? How can I get rid of this terrible disease?
How can I stop this onrushing torrent? How can I get
out of the mesh in which I find myself? If there is a way,
how can I find it?"

We have already seen that the Bible teaches that God
was a God of love. He wanted to do something for man.
He wanted to save man. He wanted to free man from the
curse of sin. How could He do it? God was a just God.
He was righteous, and holy. He had warned man from
the beginning that if he obeyed the Devil and disobeyed
God, he would die physically and spiritually. Man deliberately disobeyed God. Man had to die or God would
have been a liar, for God could not break His word. His
very nature would not allow Him to lie. His word had to
be kept. Therefore, when man deliberately disobeyed
Him, he was banished from the presence of God. He deliberately chose to go the Devil's way. God could not
freely forgive man's sin, or God would have found Himself in the impossible position of lying, because He had

said, "In the day that thou eatest thereof, thou shalt surely die." [1]

There had to be some other way, for man was help-lessly lost and hopelessly involved. Man's very nature was inverted. He opposed God. Many even denied that God existed, so blinded were they by the disease from which they suffered.

But even in the Garden of Eden, God gave a hint that He was going to do something about it. He warned the Devil and promised man, "And I will put enmity between thee and the woman, and between thy seed and her seed; it shall bruise thy head, and thou shalt bruise his heel." [2] *"And thou shalt bruise his heel"*—here was a brilliant flash of light from heaven. Here was a promise. Here was something that man could hold on to. God was promis-ing that someday a Redeemer would come, a Deliverer would come. God gave man hope. Down through the centuries man held on to that one bit of hope!

That was not all. There were other occasions through the thousands of years of history when other flashes of light came from heaven. All through the Old Testament, God gave man the promise of salvation if by faith he would believe in the coming Redeemer. Therefore God began to teach His people that man could only be saved by substitution. Someone else would have to pay the bill for man's redemption.

Go back again with me in your imagination to Eden for a moment. God said, "In the day that thou eatest thereof thou shalt surely die." Man did eat of it. He died.

Suppose that God had said, "Adam, you must have made a mistake, that was a slight error on your part. You are forgiven. Please don't do it again." God would have been a liar. He would not have been holy, neither would He have been just. He was forced by His very nature to keep His word. God's justice was at stake. Man had to die spiritually and physically. His iniquities had separated him from his God. Thus man had to suffer. He had to pay for his own sins. As we have seen, Adam was the

---

[1] *Genesis 2:17.*   [2] *Genesis 3:15.*

federal head of the human race. When Adam sinned, we all sinned. "Wherefore, as by one man sin entered into the world and death by sin; and so death passed upon all men, for that all have sinned." [3]

The burning question became "How can God be just and still justify the sinner?" It must be remembered that the word *justify* means the "clearance of the soul from guilt." Justification is far more than just forgiveness. Sin must be put away and made as though it had never been. Man must be restored so that there shall be no spot or blemish or stain. In other words, man must be taken back to the position he had before he fell from grace.

For centuries men in their blindness have been trying to get back to Eden—but they have never been able to reach their goal. They have tried many paths, but they have all failed. Education is necessary, but education will not bring a man back to God. False religions are an opiate which keep men from present misery while on their way to future glory, but they will never bring man to the place of his goal. The United Nations may be a practical necessity in a world of men of war, and we are thankful for every step that can be taken in the field of international relations that can settle disputes without recourse to war; but if the United Nations could bring lasting peace, man could say to God, "We do not need You any more. We have brought peace on earth and have organized humanity in righteousness." All of these schemes are patchwork remedies that the world must use while waiting for the Great Physician. Back in history we know that the first attempt of united man ended with the confusion of tongues at the Tower of Babel. Men have failed on every other occasion when they have tried to work without God, and they must be doomed to such failures.

The question remains "How can God be just—that is, true to Himself in nature and true to Himself in holiness, and yet justify the sinner?" Because each man had to bear his own sins, all mankind was excluded from helping,

[3] *Romans 5:12.*

since each was contaminated with the same disease.

The only solution was for an innocent party to volunteer to die physically and spiritually as a substitution before God. This innocent party would have to take man's judgment, penalty, and death. But where was such an individual? Certainly there was none on earth, for the Bible says, "All have sinned." [4] There was only one possibility. God's own Son was the only personality in the universe who had the capacity to bear in His own body the sins of the world. Certainly Gabriel might possibly have come and died for one person, but only God's Son was infinite and thus able to die for all.

The Bible teaches that God is actually three Persons. This is a mystery that we will never be able to understand. The Bible does not teach that there are three Gods—but that there is one God. This one God, however, is expressed in three Persons. There is God the Father, God the Son, and God the Spirit.

The Second Person of this Trinity is God's Son, Jesus Christ. He is co-equal with God the Father. He was not *a* Son of God but *the* Son of God. He is the Eternal Son of God—the Second Person of the Holy Trinity, God manifested in the flesh, the living Savior.

The Bible teaches that Jesus Christ had no beginning. He was never created. The Bible teaches that the heavens were created by Him. All the myriads of stars and flaming suns were created by Him. The earth was flung from His flaming finger tip. The birth of Jesus Christ that we celebrate at Christmas time was not His beginning. His origin is shrouded in that same mystery that baffles us when we inquire into the beginning of God. The Bible only tells us, "In the beginning was the Word, and the Word was with God, and the Word was God." [5]

The Bible teaches us, "Who is the image of the invisible God, the firstborn of every creature: For by Him were all things created, that are in heaven, and that are in earth, visible and invisible, whether they be thrones, or dominions, or principalities, or powers: all things were created

[4] *Romans 3:23.*   [5] *John 1:1.*

by Him, and for Him: And He is before all things, and
by Him all things consist." [6]

That last phrase indicates that He holds all things together. In other words, the entire universe would smash
into billions of atoms were it not for the cohesive power
of Jesus Christ. The Bible again says, "And, Thou, Lord,
in the beginning hast laid the foundation of the earth;
and the heavens are the works of Thine hands: They
shall perish; but Thou remainest; and they all shall wax
old as doth a garment; And as a vesture shalt Thou fold
them up, and they shall be changed: but Thou art the
same, and Thy years shall not fail." [7]

Again Jesus said of Himself, "I am Alpha and Omega,
the beginning and the end." He, and He alone, had the
power and capacity to bring man back to God. But would
He? If He did, He would have to come to earth. He
would have to take the form of a servant. He would have
to be made in the likeness of men. He would have to
humble Himself and become obedient unto death. He
would have to grapple with sin. He would have to meet
and overcome Satan, the enemy of man's soul. He would
have to buy sinners out of the slave market of sin. He
would have to loose the bonds and set the prisoners free
by paying a price—that price would be His own blood.
He would have to be despised and rejected of men, a
man of sorrows and acquainted with grief. He would
have to be smitten of God and separated from God. He
would have to be wounded for the transgressions of men
and bruised for their iniquities. He would have to reconcile God and man. He would be the great Mediator of
history. He would have to be a substitute. He would have
to die in the place of sinful man. All this would have to
be done, voluntarily.

Thanks be unto God—that is exactly what happened!
Looking down over the battlements of heaven He saw
this planet swinging in space—doomed, damned, crushed,
and bound for hell. He saw you and me struggling beneath our load of sin and bound in the chains and ropes

[6] *Colossians 1:15-17.*   [7] *Hebrews 1:10-12.*

of sin. He made His decision in the council halls of God. The angelic hosts bowed in humility and awe as heaven's Prince of Princes and Lord of Lords, who could speak worlds into space, got into His jeweled chariot, went through pearly gates, across the steep of the skies, and on a black Judean night, while the stars sang together and the escorting angels chanted His praises, stepped out of the chariot, threw off His robes, and became man!

It was as though I, while walking along a road, stepped on an anthill. I might look down and say to the ants, "I am terribly sorry that I've stepped on your anthill. I've disrupted your home. Everything is in confusion. I wish I could tell you that I loved you, that I did not mean to do it, that I would like to help you."

But you say, "That's absurd, that's impossible, ants cannot understand your language!" That's just it! How wonderful it would be if I could only become an ant for a few moments and in their own language tell them of my love for them!

That, in effect, is what Christ did. He came to reveal God to men. He it is who told us that God loves us and is interested in our lives. He it is who told us of the mercy and long-suffering and grace of God. He it is who promised life everlasting.

But more than that, Jesus Christ partook of flesh and blood in order that He might die.[8] "He was manifested to take away our sins." [9] Christ came into this world "to give His life a ransom for many." [10] The very purpose of Christ's coming into the world was that He might offer up His life as a sacrifice for the sins of men. He came to die. The shadow of His death hung like a pall over all of His thirty-three years.

The night Jesus was born Satan trembled. He sought to slay Him before He was born, and tried to slay Him as soon as He was born. When the decree went forth from Herod ordering the slaughter of all the children, its one purpose was to make certain of the death of Jesus.

[8] *Hebrews 2:14.*
[9] *1 John 3:5.*
[10] *Matthew 20:28.*

All the days of His life on earth He never once committed a sin. He is the only man who ever lived that was sinless. He could stand in front of men and say, "Which of you convinceth me of sin?" [11] He was hounded by the enemy day and night, but they never found any sin in Him. He was without spot or blemish.

Jesus lived a humble life. He made Himself of no reputation. He received no honor of men. He was born in a stable. He was reared in the insignificant village of Nazareth. He was a carpenter. He gathered around Him a humble group of fishermen as His followers. He walked among men as a man. He put on no superior air and sought no worldly preferment. He humbled Himself as no other man has ever humbled himself.

Jesus taught with such authority that the people of His day said, "Never man spake like this man." [12] Every word that He spoke was historically true. Every word that He spoke was scientifically true. Every word that He spoke was ethically true. There were no loopholes in the moral conceptions and statements of Jesus Christ. His ethical vision was wholly correct, correct in the age in which He lived and correct in every age that has followed it.

The words of this blessed Person were prophetically true. He prophesied many things that are even yet in the future. Lawyers tried to catch Him with test questions, but they could never confuse Him. His answers to His opponents were clear and clean-cut. There were no question marks about His statements, no vaguenesses in His meaning, no hesitancy in His words. He knew, and therefore spoke with quiet authority. He spoke with such simplicity that the common people heard Him gladly. Though His words were profound, yet they were plain. His words were weighty, but easily understood. They shone with a luster and simplicity of statement that staggered His enemies. He dealt with the great questions of the day in such a way that a wayfaring man had no difficulty in following Him.

The Lord Jesus cured the sick, the lame, the halt, and

[11] *John 8:46.*   [12] *John 7:46.*

the blind. He healed the leper and raised the dead. He cast out demons. He quieted the elements. He stilled the storms. He brought peace, joy, and hope to the thousands to whom He ministered.

He showed no sign of fear. He was never in a hurry. He met with no accidents. He moved with perfect coordination and precision. He had supreme poise of bearing. He did not waver or worry about His work.

He stood before Pilate and quietly said, "Thou couldst have no power at all against me, except it were given thee from above." [13] He told the frightened people that angelic legions were at His command.

He approached His cross with dignity and calmness, with an assurance and a set purpose that fulfilled the prophecy written about Him eight hundred years earlier: "He is brought as a lamb to the slaughter, and as a sheep before her shearers is dumb, so He openeth not His mouth." [14]

He moved supremely, gloriously, and with great anticipation toward the mission that He had come to accomplish. He had come to save sinful men. He had come to appease the wrath of God. He had come to buy men from the slave market of the Devil. He had come to defeat the Devil forever. He had come to conquer hell and the grave. There was only one way that He could do it. There was only one course set before Him.

His death had been prophesied thousands of years before. First, as we have seen, in Eden's Garden; and then in sermon, story, and prophecy the death of Christ was set forth in the ages past. Abraham foresaw His death as the lamb was slain. The children of Israel symbolized His death in the slaughtered lamb. Every time blood was shed on a Jewish altar it represented the Lamb of God who was someday to come and take away sin. David prophesied His death in detail in more than one prophetic Psalm. Isaiah gave whole chapters to predicting the details of His death.

Jesus Christ said that He had power to lay down His

[13] *John 19:11.*   [14] *Isaiah 53:7.*

life when He said, "The good shepherd giveth his life for the sheep." [15] He said again, "Even so must the Son of man be lifted up: That whosoever believeth in him should not perish." [16] Jesus Christ had faced the possibility of the cross far back in eternity. During all the ages which preceded His birth, He knew that the day of His death was hastening on. When He was born of a virgin, He was born with the cross darkening His pathway. He had taken on a human body in order that He might die. From the cradle to the cross, His purpose was to die.

He suffered as no man has ever suffered: "The night watches in Gethsemane, lighted by the flaming torches, the kiss of the traitor, the arrest, the trial before the high priest, the hour of waiting, the palace of the Roman governor, the journey to the palace of Herod, the rough handling by Herod's brutal soldiers, the awesome scenes while Pilate tried to save Him as priests and people clamored for His blood, the scourging, the howling multitudes, the path from Jerusalem to Golgotha, the nails in His hands, the spike through His feet, the crown of thorns upon His brow, the sarcastic and mocking cries of the two thieves on either side, 'You have saved others, now save yourself.'"

Sometimes people have asked me why Christ died so quickly, in six hours, on the cross, while other victims have agonized on the cross for two and three days. He was weak and exhausted when He came there. He had been scourged, He was physically depleted. But when Christ died, He died voluntarily. He chose the exact moment when He expired.

There He hung naked between heaven and earth. They had pulled His beard until His face bled. They had spat in His face until His face was running with the spittle of angry men. He voiced neither complaint nor appeal but simply a statement by which He let us know in two words something of the terrible physical pain He suffered when He said, "I thirst." The blood was being extracted. God demands death, either for the sinner or a substitute.

[15] John 10:11.   [16] John 3:14,15.

Christ was the substitute! Gabriel and ten legions of angels hovered on the rim of the universe, their swords unsheathed. One look from His blessed face and they would have swept the angry, shouting multitudes into hell. The spikes never held Him—it was the cords of love that bound tighter than any nails that men could mold. "But God commendeth His love toward us, in that, while we were yet sinners, Christ died for us." [17]

For you! For me! He bore our sins in His body upon the tree. As someone has said, "Behold Him on the Cross, bending His sacred head, and gathering into His heart in the awful isolation of separation from God the issue of the sin of the world, and see how out of that acceptance of the issue of sin He creates that which He does not require for Himself that He may distribute to those whose place He has taken." Standing overwhelmed in the presence of this suffering, feeling our own inability to understand or explain, and with a great sense of might and majesty overwhelming us, we hear the next words that pass His lips, "It is finished."

But the physical suffering of Jesus Christ was not the real suffering. Many men before Him had died. Many men had become martyrs. The awful suffering of Jesus Christ was His spiritual death. He reached the final issue of sin, fathomed the deepest sorrow, when God turned His back and hid His face so that He cried, "My God, why hast Thou forsaken me?" Alone in the supreme hour of mankind's history Christ uttered these words! Light blazed forth to give us a glimpse of what He was enduring, but the light was so blinding, as G. Campbell Morgan says, "that no eye could bear to gaze." The words were uttered, as Dr. Morgan has so well expressed it, "that man may know how much there is that may not be known."

He who knew no sin was made to be sin on our behalf that we might become the righteousness of God in Him. On the cross He was made sin. He was God-forsaken. Because He knew no sin there is a value beyond com-

[17] *Romans 5:8.*

prehension in the penalty He bore, a penalty that He did not need for Himself. If in bearing sin in His own body He created a value that He did not need for Himself, for whom was the value created?

How it was accomplished in the depth of the darkness man will never know. I know only one thing—He bore my sins in His body upon the tree. He stood where I should have stood. The pains of hell that were my portion were heaped on Him, and I am able to go to heaven and merit that which is not my own, but is His by every right. "All the types, the offerings, the shadows, and the symbols of the Old Testament were now fulfilled. No longer do the priests have to enter once a year into the Holiest Place. The sacrifice was penal, substitutionary, redemptive, propitiatory, reconciliatory, efficacious, and 'as it is appointed unto men once to die, but after this the judgment, so Christ was once offered to bear the sins of many.'"

Now that the ground of redemption has been laid, all the guilty sinner has to do is believe on the Son, and he can have Peace with God. "For God so loved the world, that He gave His only begotten Son, that whosoever believeth in Him should not perish, but have everlasting life." [18]

In the cross of Christ I see three things: First, a description of the depth of *man's sin*. Do not blame the people of that day for putting Christ to the cross. You and I are just as guilty. It was not the people or the Roman soldiers that put Him to the cross—it was *your* sins and *my* sins that made it necessary for Him to volunteer this death.

Second, in the cross I see the overwhelming *love of God*. If ever you should doubt the love of God, take a long, deep look at the cross, for in the cross you find the expression of God's love.

Third, in the cross is the only *way of salvation*. Jesus said, "I am the way, the truth and the life: no man cometh unto the Father but by Me." [19] There is no pos-

[18] *John 3:16.*   [19] *John 14:6.*

sibility of being saved from sin and hell, except by iden-
tifying yourself with the Christ of the cross. If there had
been any other way to save you, He would have found it.
If reformation, or living a good moral and ethical life
would have saved you, Jesus never would have died. A
substitute had to take your place. Men do not like to talk
about it. They do not like to hear about it because it
injures their pride. It takes all self out.

Many people say, "Can I not be saved by living by
the Golden Rule? Or following the precepts of Jesus? Or
living the ethical life that Jesus taught?" Even if you
could be saved by living the life that Jesus taught, you
still would be a sinner. You still would fail, because none
of you have ever lived the life that Jesus taught from
the time you were born till the time you die. You have
failed. You have transgressed. You have disobeyed. You
have sinned. Therefore, what are you going to do about
that sin? There is only one thing to do and that is to
bring it to the cross and find forgiveness.

Years ago King Charles V was loaned a large sum of
money by a merchant in Antwerp. The note came due,
but the King was bankrupt and unable to pay. The merchant gave a great banquet for the King. When all the
guests were seated and before the food was brought in,
the merchant had a large platter placed on the table before him and a fire lighted on it. Then, taking the note
out of his pocket, he held it in the flames until it was
burned to ashes. The King threw his arms around his
benefactor and wept.

Just so, we have all been mortgaged to God. The debt
was due, but we were unable to pay. Two thousand years
ago God invited the world to the Gospel feast, and in the
agonies of the cross, God held your sins and mine until
every last vestige of our guilt was consumed.

The Bible says, "Without shedding of blood is no remission." [20] Many people have said to me, "How repul-
sive! You don't mean to tell us that you believe in a
slaughterhouse religion!" Others have wondered, "I do

[20] *Hebrews* 9:22.

not understand why God demands blood." Many people have wondered, "I cannot understand why Christ had to die for me." Today the idea of the shed blood of Christ is becoming old-fashioned and out of date in a lot of preaching, but it is still there. It is in the Bible. It is the very heart of Christianity. The distinctive feature of Christianity is blood atonement. Without it we cannot be saved. Blood is actually a symbol of the death of Christ.

The Bible teaches that it first of all *redeems*. "Forasmuch as ye know that ye were not redeemed with corruptible things, as silver and gold, from your vain conversation received by tradition from your fathers; But with the precious blood of Christ, as of a lamb without blemish and without spot." [21] Not only are we redeemed from the hands of the Devil, but from the hands of the law. Christ's death on the cross brings me out from under the law. The law condemned me, but Christ satisfied every claim. All the gold and silver and the precious stones of earth could never have bought me. What they could not do, the death of Christ did. Redemption means "buying back." We had been sold for nothing to the Devil, but Christ redeemed us and brought us back.

Second, it *brings us nigh*. "But now in Christ Jesus ye who sometimes were far off are made nigh by the blood of Christ." [22] When we were "aliens from the commonwealth of Israel, and strangers from the covenants of promise, having no hope, and without God in the world," Jesus Christ brought us nigh unto God. "There is therefore now no judgment to them which are in Christ Jesus." The redeemed sinner will never have to face the judgment of Almighty God. Christ has already taken his judgment.

Third, it *makes peace*. "And, having made peace through the blood of His cross, by Him to reconcile all things unto Himself; by Him, I say, whether they be things in earth, or things in heaven." [23] The world will never know peace until it finds it in the cross of Jesus

[21] *1 Peter 1:18-19.*   [22] *Ephesians 2:13.*
[23] *Colossians 1:20.*

Christ. You will never know the peace with God, peace of conscience, peace of mind, and peace of soul until you stand at the foot of the cross and identify yourself with Christ by faith. There is the secret of peace. This is peace with God.

Fourth, it *justifies*. "Much more then, being now justified by His blood, we shall be saved from wrath through Him." [24] It changes men's standing before God. It is a change from guilt and condemnation to pardon and forgiveness. The forgiven sinner is not like the discharged prisoner who has served out his term and is discharged but with no further rights of citizenship. The repentant sinner, pardoned through the blood of Jesus Christ, regains his full citizenship. "Who shall lay any thing to the charge of God's elect? It is God that justifieth. Who is he that condemneth? It is Christ that died, yea rather, that is risen again, who is even at the right hand of God, who also maketh intercession for us." [25]

Fifth, it *cleanses*. "But if we walk in the light, as He is in the light, we have fellowship one with another, and the blood of Jesus Christ His Son cleanseth us from all sin." [26] The key word in this verse is *all*. Not part of our sins, but all of them. Every lie you ever told, every mean, low-down dirty thing that you ever did, your hypocrisy, your lustful thoughts—all are cleansed by the death of Christ.

The story has often been told that years ago, in London, there was a large gathering of noted people, and among the invited guests was a famous preacher of his day, Caesar Milan. A young lady played and sang charmingly and everyone was delighted. Very graciously, tactfully, and yet boldly the preacher went up to her after the music had ceased and said, "I thought as I listened to you tonight, how tremendously the cause of Christ would be benefited if your talents were dedicated to His cause. You know, young lady, you are as much a sinner in the sight of God as a drunkard in the ditch or a harlot

[24] *Romans 5:9.* [25] *Romans 8:33-34.*
[26] *1 John 1:7.*

on scarlet street. But I'm glad to tell you that the blood of Jesus Christ, His Son, can cleanse from all sin."

The young woman snapped out a rebuke for his presumption, to which he replied, "Lady, I mean no offense. I pray God's Spirit will convict you."

They all returned to their homes. The young woman retired but could not sleep. The face of the preacher appeared before her and his words rang through her mind. At two o'clock in the morning she sprang from her bed, took a pencil and paper, and with tears dripping from her face, Charlotte Elliott wrote that famous poem:

Just as I am, without one plea, But that Thy blood was shed for me,
And that Thou bidd'st me come to Thee, O Lamb of God, I come! I come!
Just as I am, and waiting not To rid my soul of one dark blot,
To Thee, whose blood can cleanse each spot, O Lamb of God, I come! I come!

But this is not the end. We do not leave Christ hanging on a cross with blood streaming down from His hands, His side, and His feet. He is taken down and laid carefully away in a tomb. A big stone is rolled against the entrance of the tomb. Soldiers are set to guard it. All day Saturday, His followers sit gloomily and sadly in the upper room. Two have already started toward Emmaus. Fear has gripped them all. Early on that first Easter morning, Mary, Mary Magdalene, and Salome make their way to the tomb to anoint the dead body. When they arrive, they are startled to find the tomb empty. An angel is standing at the head of the tomb and asks, "Whom do you seek?" And they reply, "We seek Jesus of Nazareth." And then the angel gives the greatest, most glorious news that human ear has ever heard, "He is not here. He is risen."

Upon that great fact hangs the entire plan of the redemptive program of God. Without the resurrection there could be no salvation. Christ predicted His resurrection many times. He said on one occasion, "For as Jonah was three days and three nights in the whale's belly; so shall the Son of man be three days and three nights in the heart of the earth." As he predicted, He rose!

There are certain laws of evidence which hold in the establishment of any historic event. There must be documentation of the event in question made by reliable contemporary witnesses. There is more evidence that Jesus rose from the dead than there is that Julius Caesar ever lived or that Alexander the Great died at the age of thirty-three. It is strange that historians will accept thousands of facts for which they can produce only shreds of evidence. But in the face of the overwhelming evidence of the resurrection of Jesus Christ they cast a skeptical eye and hold intellectual doubts. The trouble with these people is that they do not want to believe. Their spiritual vision is so blinded and they are so completely prejudiced that they cannot accept the glorious fact of the resurrection of Christ on Bible testimony alone.

The resurrection meant, first, that Christ was God of very God. He was what He claimed to be. Christ was Deity in the flesh.

Second, it meant that God had accepted His atoning work on the cross of Christ, which was necessary to our salvation. "Who was delivered for our offences, and was raised again for our justification." [27]

Third, it assures mankind of a righteous judgment.

Fourth, it guarantees that our bodies also will be raised in the end. "But now is Christ risen from the dead, and become the firstfruits of them that slept." [28] The Scripture teaches that as Christians, our bodies may go to the grave but they are going to be raised on the great resurrection morning. Then will death be swallowed up in victory. As a result of the resurrection of Christ the sting of death is gone and Christ has the keys of death. He says, "I am He that liveth, and was dead; and, behold, I am alive forevermore, Amen; and have the keys of hell and

[27] Romans 4:25.   [28] 1 Corinthians 15:20.

of death." [29] And Christ promises that "Because I live, ye shall live also."

And, fifth, it means that death is abolished. The power of death has been broken and death's fear has been removed. Now we can say with the Psalmist, "Yea, though I walk through the valley of the shadow of death, I will fear no evil: for Thou art with me; Thy rod and Thy staff they comfort me." [30]

Paul looked forward to death with great anticipation as a result of the resurrection of Christ. He said, "For to me to live is Christ, and to die is gain." [31]

Without the resurrection of Christ there could be no hope for the future. The Bible promises that someday we are going to stand face to face with the resurrected Christ, and we are going to have bodies like unto His own body.

> *Face to face with Christ my Savior,*
> *Face to face, what will it be?*
> *When with rapture I behold Him,*
> *Jesus Christ who died for me.*
>
> *Face to face shall I behold Him,*
> *Far beyond the starry sky;*
> *Face to face in all His glory*
> *I shall see Him by and by.*

[29] *Revelation 1:18.*   [30] *Psalm 23:4.*
[31] *Philippians 1:21.*

Chapter Eight

HOW AND WHERE TO BEGIN

Except ye be converted, and become as little children, ye shall not enter into the kingdom of heaven.
                                                        MATTHEW 18:3.

WE NOW recognize that there is a natural principle that pulls us down to the animal plane, blinding reason, searing conscience, paralyzing will. We stand condemned by our own deeds.

God is a holy and righteous God. He cannot tolerate sin. Sin separates from God. It brings the wrath of God upon the human soul. Man has lost his moral, intellectual, and spiritual sense of God because he has lost God. He will not find God until he finds the way back to God.

The way back to God is not an intellectual way. It is not a moral way. You cannot think your way back to God because human thought-life will not co-ordinate with divine thought-life, for the carnal mind is at enmity with God. You cannot worship your way back to God because man is a spiritual rebel from God's presence. You cannot moralize your way back to God because character is vitiated with sin.

The natural question comes to you—What shall I do? Where shall I start? Where do I begin? What is my road back to God? There is only *one way* back to God. Jesus said, "Except ye be converted, and become as little children, ye shall not enter into the kingdom of heaven." Thus Jesus demanded a conversion. This is how to begin! This is where it starts! You must be converted!

There are many people who confuse conversion with the keeping of the law. The law of Moses is set forth in specific terms in the Bible and the purpose of the law is made very clear. It was not offered at any time as a panacea for the world's ills. Rather, it was given as a diagnosis of the world's ills; it outlines the reason for our trouble, not the cure. The Bible says, "Now we know that what things soever the law saith, it saith to them who are under the law: that every mouth may be stopped, and all the world may become guilty before God." [1] The law has given a revelation of man's unrighteousness, and the Bible says, "By the deeds of the law there shall no flesh be justified in His sight." [2] It is impossible to be converted by the keeping of the law. The Bible says, "By the law is the knowledge of sin." The law is a moral mirror. It condemns but does not convert. It challenges but does not change. It points the finger but does not offer mercy. There is no life in the law. There is only death, for the pronouncement of the law was, "Thou shalt die."

There are many people who say that their religion is the Sermon on the Mount, but the man or woman is yet to be born who has ever lived up to the Sermon on the Mount. The Bible says that all have sinned and come short of His glory.

Examine your own motives before you decide that you are above reproach and living a life that absolves you from all need of conversion. Look into your own heart fearlessly and honestly before you say religious conversion is all right for some but you certainly don't stand to benefit from it.

When I was preaching in Hollywood, a group of movie people asked me to talk to them about religious experiences. After my address we had a discussion period and the very first question that was asked was, "What is conversion?"

Some time later it was my privilege to address a group of political leaders in Washington. When the discussion

[1] *Romans 3:19.*   [2] *Romans 3:20.*

period started, the first question again was, "What is conversion?"

In almost every university and college group where I have led discussions, this same question is invariably asked, "What do you mean by conversion?"

Probably there are more different answers to this query than to almost any other pertaining to religion. What *is* conversion? What is involved in it? How is it accomplished? What are its effects? Why must you be converted in order to get to heaven?

The idea of conversion is certainly not unusual in our society. Any good salesman knows that he must *convert* the prospect to his particular product or way of thinking. The chief business of advertising is to *convert* the buying public from one brand to another. We speak of political leaders being *converted* from their original political philosophy and adopting a different one. During the last war, we heard a great deal about peacetime industries *converting* to war production, and most of the oil furnaces in private homes were *converted* to coal.

Actually the word *conversion* means "to turn around," "to change one's mind," "to turn back," or "to return." In the realm of religion it has been variously explained as "to repent," "to be regenerated," "to receive grace," "to experience religion," "to gain assurance."

I remember one confirmed alcoholic who came to one of the opening meetings of a campaign and said to me, "Mr. Graham, I'm not sure there's a word of truth in what you're saying, but I'm going to give your Christ a trial, and if He works even a little bit the way you say He will, I'll come back and sign up for life!"

Weeks later he told me that he didn't quite understand it, but every time he started to take a drink it seemed as though something stopped him. Christ had given him victory over his vicious habit. He returned to his family. and is now living his life for Christ. In other words, he turned around, he changed his direction, he changed his way of thinking—he had been converted!

Conversion can take many different forms. The way it is accomplished depends largely upon the individual—

his temperament, his emotional balance, his environment, and his previous conditioning and way of life. Conversion may follow a great crisis in a person's life; or it could come after all former values have been swept away, when great disappointment has been experienced, when one has lost one's sense of power through material possessions, or lost the object of one's affections. A man or woman who has been focusing all attention on financial gains, business or social prestige, or centering all affection on some one person experiences a devastating sense of loss when denied the thing that has given life its meaning.

In these tragic moments, as the individual stands stripped of all his worldly power, when the loved one is gone beyond recall, he recognizes how terribly and completely alone he really is. In that moment, the Holy Spirit may cause the worldly bandages to fall from his eyes and he sees clearly for the first time. He recognizes that God is the only source of real power, and the only enduring fountainhead of love and companionship.

Or again, conversion may take place at the very height of personal power or prosperity—when all things are going well and the bountiful mercies of God have been bestowed generously upon you. The very goodness of God can drive you to a recognition that you owe all to God; thus, the very goodness of God leads you to repentance.

Conversion at such a moment can be as sudden and dramatic as the conversion of pagans who transfer their affection and faith from idols carved of stone and wood, to the Person of Jesus Christ.

Not all conversions come as a sudden, brilliant flash of soul illumination that we call a crisis conversion. There are many others that are accomplished only after a long and difficult conflict with the inner motives of the person. With others, conversion comes as the climactic moment of a long period of gradual conviction of their need and revelation of the plan of salvation. This prolonged process results in conscious acceptance of Christ as personal Savior and in the yielding of life to Him.

We may say, therefore, that conversion can be an instantaneous event, a crisis in which the person receives a clear revelation of the love of God; or it can be a gradual unfoldment accompanied by a climactic moment at the time the line is crossed between darkness and light, between death and life everlasting.

It does not always happen in exactly this way. My wife, for example, cannot remember the exact day or hour when she became a Christian, but she is certain that there was such a moment in her life, a moment when she actually crossed the line. Many young people who have grown up in Christian homes and had the benefit of Christian training are unaware of the time when they committed their lives to Christ. Others remember very clearly when they made their public confession of faith. The reports of conversions in the New Testament indicate that most of them were the dramatic, crisis type.

For many years, psychology left conversion and religious experience alone, but in the last twenty-five years much study has been made by psychologists concerning the matter of conversion. They have pointed out that conversion is not only a Christian experience but is also found in other religions, and that it is not necessarily a religious phenomenon but also occurs in nonreligious spheres. Students of psychology have agreed that there are three steps of conversion: First, a sense of perplexity and uneasiness; second, a climax and turning point; and, third, a relaxation marked by rest and joy.

Starbuck says that there are two kinds of conversion. He says that one is accompanied by a violent sense of sin, and the other by a feeling of incompleteness, a struggle after a larger life and a desire for spiritual illumination.

The value of psychological studies of conversion has been underestimated. We cannot brush them aside and ignore them. They shed a great deal of light, but few of them are willing to accept the Biblical conversion as a supernatural experience.

Actually, Biblical conversion involves three steps—two of them active and one passive. In active conversion, repentance and faith are involved. Repentance is conversion viewed from its starting point, the turning from the former life. Faith indicates the objective point of conversion, the turning to God. The third, which is passive, we may call the new birth, or regeneration.

Now in order to get to heaven, Jesus said that you must be converted. I didn't say it—Jesus said it! This is not man's opinion—this is God's opinion! Jesus said, "Except ye be converted, and become as little children, ye shall not enter into the kingdom of heaven."

True conversion will involve the total *mind,* the total *affection,* and the total *will.* There have been thousands of people who have been intellectually converted to Christ. They believe the entire Bible. They believe all about Jesus, but they have never been really converted to Him.

In the second chapter of John there is a description of the hundreds of people who were following Jesus early in His ministry. It says that many of them believed on Him. But Jesus did not commit Himself to them because He knew the hearts of all men. Why would Jesus not commit Himself to them? He knew that they believed with their heads and not with their hearts.

There is a vast difference between intellectual conversion and the total conversion that saves the soul. To be sure, there must be a change in your thinking and intellectual acceptance of Christ.

There are thousands of people who have had some form of emotional experience that they refer to as conversion but who have never been truly converted to Christ. Christ demands a change in the way you live—and if your life does not conform to your experience, then you have every reason to doubt your experience! Certainly there will be a change in the elements that make up emotion when you come to Christ—hate and love will be involved, because you will begin to hate sin and love righteousness. Your affections will undergo a revolutionary change. Your devotion to Him will know no bounds. Your love for Him cannot be described.

But even if you have an intellectual acceptance of

Christ, and an emotional experience—that still is not enough. There must be the conversion of the will! There must be that determination to obey and follow Christ. Your *will* must be bent to the will of God. Self must be nailed to the cross. The only desire you will have will be to please Him.

In conversion as you stand at the foot of the cross, the Holy Spirit makes you realize that you are a sinner. He directs your faith to the Christ who died in your place. You must open your heart and let Him come in. At that precise moment the Holy Spirit performs the miracle of the new birth. You actually become a new moral creature. There comes the implantation of the divine nature. You become a partaker of God's own life. Jesus Christ, through the Spirit of God, takes up residence in your heart.

Conversion is so simple that the smallest child can be converted, but it is also so profound that theologians throughout history have pondered the depth of its meaning. God has made the way of salvation so plain that "the wayfaring men, though fools, shall not err therein." [3] No person will ever be barred from the kingdom of God because he did not have the capacity to understand. The rich and the poor, the sophisticated and the simple—all can be converted.

To sum it up, conversion simply means "to change." When a person is converted he may continue to love objects which he loved before, but there will be a change of *reasons* for loving them. A converted person may forsake former objects of affection. He may even withdraw from his worldly companions, not because he despises them, for many of them will be decent and amiable, but because there is more attraction for him in the fellowship of other Christians of like mind.

The converted person will love what he once hated, and hate what he once loved. There will even be a change of heart about God. Where he once may have been careless about God, living in constant fear, dread,

[3] *Isaiah* 35:8.

and antagonism to God, he now finds himself in a state of complete reverence, confidence, obedience, and devotion. There will be a reverential fear of God, a constant gratitude to God, a dependence upon God, and a new loyalty to Him. Before conversion there may have been gratification of the flesh. Culture and intellectual pursuits or the making of money may have been of first and supreme importance. Now, righteousness and holiness of heart, and living the Christian life will be placed above all other concerns, for pleasing Christ will be the only thing of real importance. In other words, conversion means a complete change in the life of an individual.

I remember so vividly a young New York career girl who came out to Los Angeles to be married. She and the young man had met when they were both working in a high-powered New York advertising agency, and their courtship had been conducted against a background of cocktail parties and night clubs. Filled with ambition and "on his way up," he had himself transferred to the California office, with the understanding that the girl would follow him in six months and they would be married.

About a week after she had arrived in Los Angeles, expecting to take up a gay new life, she discovered that the man had fallen in love with a movie starlet and lacked the courage to write her about it before she left New York!

Here she was, alone in a city where she knew no one— all her plans in ruins, her pride crushed, and the future stretching ahead, bleak and empty. Her family had not been religious, and in this hour of extreme need she knew of nowhere to turn for comfort, advice, or guidance.

As she walked along the unfamiliar streets, trying to overcome her shock and humiliation, she came upon the "canvas cathedral" in which we were conducting our campaign. She said she was never sure what made her come inside, but she did, and sat glumly through the entire service. The next night she came again, and every night for the whole week, until through the cloud of bitterness and misery that surrounded her, God made His

voice heard, and she came forward to confess her need
of salvation.

With the burden of guilt and rejection lifted from her
through faith in the Lord Jesus Christ, she came to see
that the love she had lost was but a steppingstone to a
far greater and much richer love. The sense of humiliation that prevented her from returning to her former New
York job vanished, and rather than life being finished,
she found upon her return that it was fuller than ever.
Only instead of wasting her brains and organizational
ability on an endless round of cocktail parties, she became extremely active in her church.

The imagination she formerly devoted to entertaining
the "office crowd" now goes into making Bible stories
come alive for the young people. Her training as a fund-
raiser is now being put to good use in the service of the
Lord, and her minister says her ideas have been invalu-
able in increasing regular church attendance. Far from
being rejected and unwanted, she is sought after constantly by her fellow church members. But, most important of all, her sense of loneliness has vanished, for
she knows now that Jesus Christ is ever by her side, ready
to comfort, to guide, and to protect her.

All this had come as a result of her conversion—her
turning away from the bleak, empty, worldly road she
was traveling so unhappily—to her Lord and Savior, Jesus
Christ! She had found peace with God.

Chapter Nine

REPENT

*Joy shall be in heaven over one sinner that repenteth,
more than over ninety and nine just persons which
need no repentance.*

LUKE 15:7.

WE HAVE now seen that Jesus demanded conversion.
We have also seen that the three elements of conversion
are repentance, faith, and regeneration. It may be debat-
able in which order these three should come, but it is
generally agreed that they probably happen at the same
time. Whether you are conscious or unconscious of it, in
that critical moment of conversion these three take place
simultaneously.

If repentance could be described in one word, I would
use the word *renounce*. "Renounce what?" you ask. The
answer can also be given in one word—"sin." The Bible
teaches, as we have already seen, that sin is a transgression of the law. Sin is the absence of all authority and
the denial of all obligation to God. Sin is that evil principle which came into the Garden of Eden when Adam
and Eve were tempted and fell. Ever since the disaster
in Eden this evil poison has affected all men so that "all
have sinned," and "there is none righteous, no, not one."
Sin has destroyed our relationship with God, and as a
consequence has disturbed our relationship with each
other, and even with ourselves.

We cannot possibly have peace with God or peace
with each other in the world or even peace within ourselves until something is done about that "abominable

thing which God hates." Not only are we told that we must renounce the principle of sin, but we are also to renounce *sins*—plural. We are to renounce the world, the flesh, and the Devil. There can be no parleying, bargaining, compromise, or hesitation. Christ demands absolute renunciation.

But here again the principle of love is involved, because when you fall in love completely and absolutely with Jesus Christ you will not want to do the things that He hates and abhors. You will automatically renounce all the sins of your life when you surrender by faith to Him. Therefore repentance and faith go hand in hand. You cannot have genuine repentance without saving faith, and you cannot have saving faith without genuine repentance.

The word *repentance* is sadly missing today from the average pulpit. It is a very unpopular word. The first sermon Jesus ever preached was "Repent: for the kingdom of heaven is at hand." [1] This was God speaking through His Son. Jesus had come with a heart filled with love and compassion, but He immediately began to press home man's guilt and sins. He called upon men to acknowledge their guilt and to turn from their ungodliness. He said repentance must come before He could pour out His love, grace, and mercy upon men. Jesus refused to gloss over iniquity. He insisted upon self-judgment, upon a complete right about-face. He insisted upon a new attitude before He would reveal the love of God.

The people came to Jesus one day and told Him of certain Galileans whose blood Pilate had mingled with the sacrifices as his Roman legions quelled the Jewish uprising. They reported, too, how the falling of a tower in Siloam had killed many. In answer Jesus declared, "Suppose ye that these Galileans were sinners above all the Galileans . . . I tell you, Nay: but, except ye repent, ye shall all likewise perish." [2] In other words, Jesus said whether men are taken away by violence, by accident, or by natural death, their doom is the same unless they

[1] *Matthew 4:17.*   [2] *Luke 13:3.*

have turned to God in repentance. Until this is done, faith is absolutely impossible. This does not limit the grace of God, but repentance makes way for the grace of God.

We know that salvation is based entirely upon the grace of God. We have already seen that sacrifices, ritual, or works of the law have never been able to save a single soul. The Bible says that no man is justified by the law in the sight of God. The Bible says, "The just shall live by his faith." [3] Salvation, forgiveness, and justification are based entirely upon the atoning work of Christ. However, if the sacrifice of Christ on the cross is to be made effectual for any individual of any age, that individual must repent of sin and accept Christ by faith.

Jonah preached repentance in Nineveh until Nineveh repented.

Ezekiel preached repentance when he said, "Therefore I will judge you, O house of Israel, every one according to his ways, saith the Lord God. Repent, and turn yourselves from all your transgressions; so iniquity shall not be your ruin." [4]

The great message of John the Baptist was repentance when he said, "Repent ye: for the kingdom of heaven is at hand." [5]

Repentance is mentioned seventy times in the New Testament. Jesus said, "Except ye repent, ye shall all likewise perish." The sermon that Peter preached on the Day of Pentecost was, "Repent, and be baptized every one of you in the name of Jesus Christ for the remission of sins." [6] Paul preached it when he said that he "testified both to the Jews, and also to the Greeks, repentance toward God, and faith toward our Lord Jesus Christ." [7] The Bible says God commands repentance, "And the times of this ignorance God winked at; but now commandeth all men every where to repent." [8] It is a com-

---

[3] *Romans 1:17.*   [4] *Ezekiel 18:30.*
[5] *Matthew 3:2.*   [6] *Acts 2:38.*
[7] *Acts 20:21.*   [8] *Acts 17:30.*

mand. It is an imperative. God says, "Repent! Or perish!"
Have you repented? Are you sure of it?

What did Jesus mean by the word *repent?* Why does
it appear over and over throughout the Bible? If you
look in the modern dictionary you will find that repent
means "to feel sorry for, or to regret." But the original
Greek and Hebrew words that Jesus spoke meant a great
deal more than that. It meant a great deal more than
just regretting and feeling sorry about sin. The Biblical
word *repent* means "to change, or to turn." It is a word
of power and action. It is a word that signifies a complete revolution in the individual. When the Bible calls
upon us to repent of sin, it means that we should turn
away from sin, that we should do an about-face and
walk in the opposite direction from sin and all that it
implies.

Jesus told the parable of the Prodigal Son to dramatize
what He meant by the word *repent.* When the Prodigal
Son repented he didn't just sit still and feel sorry about
all his sins. He wasn't passive and limp about it. He didn't
stay where he was, surrounded by the swine. He got up
and left! He turned his feet in the other direction. He
sought out his father and humbled himself before him,
and then he got his reward.

Too many modern Christians have lost sight of what
the Bible means when it talks about repentance. They
think that repentance is little more than shaking their
heads over their sins and saying, "My, but I'm sorry I did
that!" and then continuing to live just as they have lived
before.

True repentance means "to change, to turn away from,
to go in a new direction." To be sorry is not enough in
repentance. Judas was remorseful and sorry, but he never
repented. Even reformation is not enough. There is no
torture that you can give your body, no trials you can set
for your mind that will be pleasing to Almighty God.
Our sins were atoned for by Christ on the cross. There
He suffered sin's penalty. No suffering that we can undergo will lead us to repentance.

When I speak of repentance I am not speaking of the

old-time mourners' bench. Many people have taught that
in order to repent you must mourn for a stated time in
order to be ready for salvation. One man told me the
night he found Christ he went forward in an old-
fashioned camp meeting some years ago. While he was
kneeling at the altar trying to find God, some dear sister
came and slapped him on the back and said, "Hold on,
brother! If you want God, you'll have to hold on." A few
minutes later a church officer came up and slapped him
across the back and said, "Brother, turn loose!" Then another sister came up a few minutes later and said, "The
night I was converted a big light hit me in the face and
knocked me cold." He said, "I tried to turn loose and
hold on at the same time while looking for the light. I
almost never made it in the confusion!"

A very intelligent Christian leader once told me that
at the time he was converted the demonstration of emotion expected of him by the preacher and congregation
almost kept him from coming to God.

Falsely produced emotionalism in some revival meetings has been a stumbling block to many a sincere,
searching soul. But the type of repentance I'm talking
about is true Biblical repentance, which involves three
things: it involves the *intellect*, the *emotion*, and the
will.

First, there must be a *knowledge* of sin. The Bible
says, "All have sinned, and come short of the glory of
God." [9] When Isaiah was convicted of his sins he said,
"Woe is me! . . . I am a man of unclean lips." [10] When
Job was convinced that he was a sinner he said, "I abhor
myself." [11] When Peter was convicted of his sins he said,
"I am a sinful man." [12] When Paul was convicted of his
sins he called himself "the chief of sinners."

It is the Holy Spirit that brings about this conviction.
Actually, repentance cannot take place unless first there
is a movement of the Holy Spirit in the heart and mind.
The Holy Spirit may use a mother's prayers, a pastor's

[9] *Romans* 3:23.   [10] *Isaiah* 6:5.
[11] *Job* 42:6.   [12] *Luke* 5:8.

sermon, a Christian radio program, the sight of a church steeple, or the death of a loved one to bring about this necessary conviction. However, I have seen men in some of our meetings stand trembling under conviction and still not repent of their sins. It is possible to be convicted of sin and know you are a sinner and even shed tears over your sins, and yet not repent.

Second, the *emotions* are involved in repentance, just as they are in all genuine experiences. Paul said there is a godly sorrow that worketh toward repentance. "Many people abhor all emotion, and some critics are suspicious of any conversion that does not take place in a refrigerator. There are many dangers in false emotionalism, produced for its own effect, but that does not rule out true emotion and depth of feeling."

As Dr. W. E. Sangster, the great British Methodist preacher, says in his book *Let Me Commend*, "The man who screams at a football or baseball game but is distressed when he hears of a sinner weeping at the cross and murmurs something about the dangers of emotionalism hardly merits intelligent respect."

Horace Walpole once accused John Wesley of acting out very ugly emotionalism in his preaching.

Third, repentance involves the *will*.

It is only when we come to the *will* that we find the very heart of repentance. There must be that determination to forsake sin—to change one's attitudes toward self, toward sin, and God; to change one's feeling; to change one's will, disposition, and purpose.

Only the Spirit of God can give you the determination necessary for true repentance. It means more than the little girl who prayed, "Make me good—not real good, but good enough so I won't get whipped."

We have hundreds of people in America who have their names on church rolls. They go to church when it is convenient. They give their money to the church and support its activities. They shake hands with the minister after the service and tell him what a splendid sermon he preached. They may talk the language of the Christian and many of them can quote a fair amount of Scripture, but they have never really experienced true repentance. They have a sort of "take-it-or-leave-it-alone" attitude toward religion. They turn to God and pray when they get in a tight place, but the rest of the time they do not give God very much thought. The Bible teaches that when a person comes to Christ a change takes place that is reflected in everything he does.

There is not one verse of Scripture that indicates you can be a Christian and live any kind of a life you want to. When Christ enters into the human heart, He demands that He be Lord and Master. He demands complete surrender. He demands control of your intellectual processes. He demands that your body be subject to Him, and to Him alone. He demands your talents and abilities. He demands all your work and labor be performed in His name.

Too many of today's professing Christians would give up going to church before they would give up getting a new refrigerator. Given a choice between making the down payment on a new car or contributing to the building of a new Sunday school, it is easy to guess what the decision of many would be. Thousands of so-called Christians are putting money and the things that make up our high standard of living ahead of the teachings of Christ. We can find time for the movies, baseball games, or prize fights but we can't find time for God. We can save toward a new home or a bigger television set, but we feel we no longer can afford to tithe. This is idolatry.

A change must take place! We point our fingers at the heathen and at the idol worshipers of old, but the only difference is that our graven images are made of gleaming chromium and steel and have thermostats and defrosting devices instead of jeweled eyes! Instead of gold, their surfaces are covered with easy-to-clean lifetime porcelain, but we worship them just the same, and feel that our lives would be impossible without them.

Jesus demands Lordship over all such things. He wants you to yield everything concerning your social life, your family life, your business life to Him. He must have first place in everything you do or think or say, for when you truly repent you turn toward God in everything.

We have the warning of Christ that He will not receive us into His kingdom until we are ready to give up all, until we are ready to turn from all sin in our lives. Don't try to do it part way. Don't say, "I'll give up some of my sins and hang on to some others. I'll live part of my life for Jesus and part for my own desires." Jesus demands one hundred per cent surrender, and when that is accomplished He rewards a thousandfold. But don't expect Jesus to hand out any small size five hundred per cent awards for fifty per cent surrenders! God doesn't work that way His wonders to perform! He demands a total change, a total surrender. When you have determined that you are renouncing sin, forsaking sin, and yielding all to Christ, you have taken another step toward peace with God.

Chapter Ten

FAITH

For by grace are ye saved through faith; and not of yourselves: it is the gift of God: not of works, lest any man should boast.

EPHESIANS 2:8,9.

WE ARE now ready to take up the next step in finding peace with God. You are now ready to forsake your past life and your sins. You are determined that this change is going to take place in your life. You are no longer headed away from God, but you are moving toward His love and mercy and protection. You have made your decision. You have chosen your path. You have repented; you have chosen the right road, even though it may be a difficult one. You have chosen the road that Moses took almost thirty-five hundred years ago when he renounced his right to the throne of Egypt and decided in favor of God!

Moses was forty years old when he made his great decision, when he concluded that faith and truth in company with agony and hardship were better than wealth and fame and the absence of God's love. Few men in history have been called upon to make a more difficult decision than his.

Moses was a man of education and culture, a man of wealth and prominence. As the son of Pharaoh's daughter he was accustomed to every honor, every luxury, and every privilege. The throne of Egypt, richest, most powerful, most spectacularly romantic country of its time, was within his grasp.

Yet the Bible records that "By faith Moses, when he

108

was come to years, refused to be called the son of Pharaoh's daughter; Choosing rather to suffer affliction with the people of God, than to enjoy the pleasures of sin for a season; Esteeming the reproach of Christ greater riches than the treasures in Egypt: for he had respect unto the recompense of the reward. By faith he forsook Egypt, not fearing the wrath of the king: for he endured, as seeing Him who is invisible." [1]

Notice, it says that he "refused" and he "forsook"—this is true repentance. And then it says he did it "by faith"! This is the next step—*faith*. Moses made this decision not in a moment of overt emotionalism that some psychologists insist is necessary for religious experience. He was not motivated by frustration. He was not a hopeless misfit or an unfulfilled man. Moses was not choosing the path of God as a compensation for the rewards that he felt life had withheld from him, nor was he turning to the religious life out of boredom and apathy. He did not want for interest, entertainment, and amusement.

None of these arguments, or the many others so often advanced as reasons for seeking life with God, were valid in the case of Moses. He was not forced to run from the flesh and the Devil. He did it from choice. Moses was certainly neither weak-minded nor weak-willed. He was not a child clinging to the security of an established order. He was not a nonentity seeking recognition and prestige. He was not any of the things that those who mock religion say one must be to feel the need of salvation. Moses had even more than the dreams to which most men would aspire; and yet out of his mature judgment in the prime of life he turned his back on wealth, position, and esteem and chose instead faith in God.

Every time I hear it said that only the hopeless and helpless, only the maladjusted need the comfort of religion, I think of Moses.

It has been my privilege to talk to hundreds of thousands of men and women concerning their spiritual problems. I have learned that when men and women of sound

[1] *Hebrews 11:24-27.*

judgment reject Christ as their Lord and Master, they do it not because they find Christian doctrines intellectually distasteful, but because they seek to avoid the responsibilities and obligations that the Christian life demands. It is their faint hearts rather than their brilliant minds that stand between them and Christ. They are not willing to submit themselves and surrender everything to Christ.

Moses considered the claims and obligations of religion carefully. He realized that if he was to embrace God he would have to do it at the sacrifice of the things that men usually hold most dear. He made no hasty examination. He came to no half-considered conclusions under sudden impulse or emotional reaction. He knew how much was at stake and he arrived at his decision with the full use of his well-trained and superior mental faculties. His final choice was not in the nature of a temporary experiment. He did not select faith as a tentative measure. It was a mature conviction with an unalterable purpose, a conviction not to be shaken by changes of fortune or the trials of long-endured privation. He carefully burned all the bridges and ships that might have made retreat possible from his new position. When Moses had his great crisis moment at the age of forty, he committed himself without reservation for all time and under all circumstances to God and His commands.

How different was the quality of Moses' decision from that of the famous biographer Gamaliel Bradford, who, as he neared the end of his life, said, "I do not dare read the New Testament for fear of awakening a storm of anxiety and doubt and dread, of having taken the wrong path, of having been a traitor to the plain and simple God."

Moses had no such fear. And neither should you fear if you turn yourself wholeheartedly to Christ now and forever *by faith*. Don't turn to Him saying, "I'll try Christianity for a while. If it works I'll go on with it, but if it doesn't I still have time to choose another way of life." When you come to Christ, every bridge has to be burned behind you, with no thought of ever turning back.

Years ago, when the wings of the fierce Roman eagle

cast an ominous shadow over the world, those audacious warriors whom Caesar led sallied forth to conquer Britain. As the enemy vessels appeared on the horizon, thousands of Englishmen bravely gathered on the heights to defend their homeland. To their utter bewilderment, the first thing the Romans did on disembarking was to set fire to their ships. When the wild flames consumed the craft, the only avenue of retreat was cut off for the daring invaders. With such an indomitable spirit, how could they fail to conquer! Little wonder the petty village on the banks of the Tiber became the Mistress of the world!

Just so, Christ demands absolute surrender and devotion. "And Jesus said unto him, No man, having put his hand to the plow, and looking back, is fit for the kingdom of God." [2]

Moses made his soul-shaking choice as he stood at the fork of life's highway. His judicial mind weighed all the facts that bore upon his decision. He looked long and carefully down each road to its termination. He considered all the pros and cons and only then did he decide to put his trust and faith in God.

First he looked down the broad road, the bright road filled with power and luxury, filled with gaiety and wine, rich in the things the world counts as pleasure. It was a familiar road. He knew it well. He had traveled it for forty years and he knew that it ended in destruction, knew that it could only lead to hell.

Then Moses looked down the other road, the narrow road, the more difficult road. He saw the suffering, the affliction, the humiliation, and disappointment. He saw the hardships and the trials, the sorrows and the pains, but *by faith* he saw also the triumphs and the reward of eternal life.

A man of lesser judgment, a man of lesser experience than Moses, might have been tempted to take the first road. Egypt was then the greatest power on earth. It held command of the fertile Nile Valley, the granary of the world. Its armies were invincible, its colleges and univer-

[2] *Luke 9:62.*

sities were setting the pattern that other centuries would follow.

Few of us are ever asked to give up as much for God as Moses did. Few of us are ever shown temptation in such abundance and variety and asked to withstand it. Few of us have such earthly delights and pleasures spread before our eyes, and even the Scriptures admit that there is pleasure in sin, if only for a season. The pleasure is fleeting and leaves no comfort in its wake.

In choosing God, Moses made a great sacrifice, but he also won a great reward. Great fortunes were rare in Moses' time, and few men indeed had the opportunity that he had to become the wealthiest man on earth.

Today, many men can amass great fortunes. In 1923 (when fortune gathering was this country's major interest) a group of the world's most successful financiers gathered at the Edgewater Beach Hotel in Chicago. Even in the fabulous twenties, the meeting was an impressive array of wealth and power. Seated at a single table were the president of the world's largest independent steel company, the president of the largest utility company, a great wheat speculator, the president of the New York Stock Exchange, a member of the cabinet of the President of the United States, the president of the Bank of International Settlements, the man who was known as the biggest trader on Wall Street, and another who headed the world's most powerful monopoly. Together, these eight men controlled more wealth than the United States Treasury! Their success stories were known to every schoolboy. They were the models that other men tried to copy. They were the financial and industrial giants of America!

In 1923 the widely publicized stories of these men were glamorous and exciting. They fired the imagination! They kindled envy! They inspired other men to try to be as they were! But in 1923 their stories were only half told —the closing chapters were yet to be written.

At the time these eight men sat down together at the hotel in Chicago they were each at the place in their individual lives where Moses had been when he stood at the crossroads. These men were at the crossroads too, and two paths stretched out before each of them. Perhaps they were paths they could not see, paths about which they did not care. Certainly they were paths they didn't choose to follow, and today their stories are complete. Today we know those final chapters. We can review their lives, just as we can review the life of Moses, and see which seems the wisest and the best.

Charles Schwab, president of the steel company, lived the last years of his life on borrowed money and died penniless. Arthur Cutten, greatest of the wheat speculators, died abroad insolvent. Richard Whitney, president of the New York Stock Exchange, served a term in Sing-Sing Penitentiary. Albert Paul, the cabinet member, was pardoned from prison so he could die at home. Jesse Livermore, the "bear" of Wall Street; Leon Frazer, president of the Bank of International Settlements, and Ivar Kreuger, head of the world's largest monopoly, all committed suicide!

These men all had money, power, fame, prestige, intelligence, and education—but every one of them lacked the one attribute that gives life its real meaning and purpose. They lacked the one attribute that is essential to the Christian creed and conduct—the attribute that makes conversion possible, that makes regeneration real. They refused to believe!

These men had no faith, or if they did have faith, they refused to act upon it. How different the closing chapters of their lives would have been if they had been able to count faith in Christ among their treasures.

Notice that it was through *faith* that Moses renounced the wealth of Egypt. It was his *faith* that made him know that even though he might suffer privation and humiliation all the rest of his life on earth, in the end he would receive the greatest of rewards—eternal life.

Men like Cutten and Schwab might have thought Moses a fool. They would have said, "A bird in the hand is worth far more than two in the bush." They would have said, "Look, you know what you have in Egypt. You know what a man of your brains can do to manipulate this wealth and power. Play your cards right and Egypt will control the world. You can put all the lesser countries out of business. You can get rid of all the competition and run things your own way." That's what they would have said, because that's the way they thought, that's the way they operated, that's the way many of them amassed their fortunes. They would have laughed at a person who said he believed God or had faith in Christ. They would have said, "Faith isn't good business. It isn't smart."

The Bible teaches that *faith* is the only approach to God. "For he that cometh to God must *believe* that He is, and that He is a rewarder of them that diligently seek Him." [3] The Bible also teaches that faith pleases God more than anything else. "Without *faith* it is impossible to please Him." [4]

People all over the world torture themselves, clothe themselves in strange garments, disfigure their bodies, deny themselves the necessities of life, spend much time in prayer and self-sacrifice in an effort to make themselves acceptable in God's sight. This may be all well and good, but the greatest thing we can do to please God is to *believe* Him.

I might go to a friend and flatter him, but, if after all my flowery phrases I were to tell him that I did not believe him, every flattering thing I said would have been in vain. I would have built him up only to let him down.

The greatest way we can please God is to *believe* His Word. It would seem that Christ was almost pleading for faith on the part of His hearers when He said, "Believe Me that I am in the Father, and the Father in Me: or else believe Me for the very works' sake." [5]

The Bible declares that *faith* is absolutely essential. You ask, "Well, if faith is so important, what is faith? What do you mean by faith? What is a definition of faith? How can I know if I have proper faith? How much faith must I have?"

[3] *Hebrews 11:6.*   [4] *Hebrews 11:6.*
[5] *John 14:11.*

Wait just a minute—not so many questions at a time! I'll try to answer them as we go along.

The Bible teaches, time and time again, that we can have salvation only through faith:

"*Believe* on the Lord Jesus Christ, and thou shalt be saved, and thy house." [6]

"But as many as received Him, to them gave He power to become the sons of God, even to them that *believe* on His name." [7]

"And by Him all that *believe* are justified from all things, from which ye could not be justified by the law of Moses." [8]

"But to him that worketh not, but *believeth* on Him that justifieth the ungodly, his faith is counted for righteousness." [9]

"Therefore being justified by *faith*, we have peace with God through our Lord Jesus Christ." [10]

"But we are not of them who draw back unto perdition; but of them that *believe* to the saving of the soul." [11]

"For by grace are ye saved through *faith;* and that not of yourselves: it is the gift of God." [12]

Are we actually saved by faith? No, we're saved by grace *through faith*. Faith is simply the channel through which God's grace to us is received. It is the hand that reaches out and receives the gift of His love. In Hebrews 11:1, we read, "Now faith is the substance of things hoped for, the evidence of things not seen." Weymouth has translated it this way, which makes it easier to understand, "Now faith is a confident assurance of that for which we hope, a conviction of the reality of things which we do not see." Faith literally means "to give up, surrender, or commit." Faith is utter confidence.

I have never been to the North Pole, and yet I believe there is a North Pole. How do I know? I know because somebody told me. I read about it in a history book, I

[6] *Acts 16:31.*   [7] *John 1:12.*
[8] *Acts 13:39.*   [9] *Romans 4:5.*
[10] *Romans 5:1.*   [11] *Hebrews 10:39.*
[12] *Ephesians 2:8.*

saw a map in a geography book and I believe the men who wrote those books. I accept it by faith.

The Bible says, "Faith cometh by hearing, and hearing by the word of God." [13] We believe what God has to say about salvation. We accept it without question.

Martin Luther has translated Hebrews 11:27 this way, "For he held on to Him whom he saw not just as though he saw Him."

It is not some peculiar, mysterious quality for which we must strive. Jesus said we must become as little children, and just as little children trust their parents, so we must trust God.

Suppose I were driving along the road at fifty miles an hour and I came to the crest of a hill. Would I immediately slam on my brakes, stop my car, get out, walk up to the top of the hill, and look over to see if the road continues? No, I wouldn't do that. I would trust the highway department of the particular state in which I was driving. I would continue at my normal rate of speed, secure in the knowledge that the road continued on ahead even though I couldn't see it. I would accept it on faith. So it is with saving faith in Christ!

Again, as in repentance, there are three things that are involved in faith. First, there must be a *knowledge* of what God has said. That's why it's so important for you to read the Bible. That's why it's important for you to know something of the teaching of the Bible concerning the salvation of the soul. Just to know that you are a sinner and that Christ died for you is enough knowledge. Knowing no more than John 3:16 could be enough knowledge. Many have been converted on less. But on anything as important as this you should be as well informed as possible and the only place to learn about salvation is in the Bible!

Many people say, "But I cannot understand much of the Bible, therefore I don't try to read it." That is not the wise attitude. There are many things in the Bible that I do not understand. My finite mind will never understand

[13] *Romans 10:17.*

all about the infinite. I do not understand all about television, but I do not refuse to turn on my television set. I accept it by faith.

But God does not ask the impossible. He does not ask you to take a leap in the dark concerning conversion. Believing in Christ is based on the best evidence in the world, the Bible. Even though you do not understand it all, you can accept it at face value because God said it. One of the first attacks that the Devil makes on man is to get him to doubt the Word of God. If you begin doubting and putting question marks over God's Word, then you're in trouble. There must be a knowledge that you are a sinner. You must have the knowledge that Christ died for your sins and that He rose again for your justification. The death, burial, and resurrection of Jesus Christ is the very heart of the Gospel. That must be believed and accepted as a minimum for conversion.

Second, the *emotions* again are involved. The Bible says, "The fear of the Lord is the beginning of wisdom." [14] Paul said, "The love of Christ constraineth us." [15] Desire, love, fear—are all emotions. Emotion cannot be cut out of life. No intelligent person would think of saying, "Let's do away with all emotion." To remove all personality from deep feeling is impossible. We cannot imagine life without the warm overtones of feeling. Suppose we had a family where everyone acted only from a cold sense of duty. Suppose I asked my wife to marry me after I had explained to her first of all that I had no feeling for her at all.

As Dr. Sangster says, "Carry the same principle over into religion. Require that the Herald of God announce the offer of His King, freely to pardon and fully to bless, but firmly forbid that any transport of joy should accompany either the announcement of the news or its glad reception, and you ask the impossible."

There is going to be a tug at the heart. Emotion may vary in religious experience. Some people are stoical and others are demonstrative, but the feeling will be there.

[14] *Proverbs 1:7.*   [15] *2 Corinthians 5:14.*

When Churchill gave his masterful speeches to the British people during the war, he appealed to logic, but at the same time he made his audience *feel*. I remember hearing him one time at Ibrox Park in Glasgow. He tickled my brain cells, but he made me feel like standing up and shouting and waving a flag! When you fall in love with Jesus Christ your emotions are bound to be stirred.

Third, and most important of all, is the *will*. It's like three little men—one is named "Intellect," the second is named "Emotion," and the third is named "Will." Intellect says that the Gospel is logical. Emotion puts pressure upon Will and says, "I feel love for Christ," or "I feel fear of judgment." And then the middleman, called Will, is the referee. He sits there with his hand on his chin, in deep thought, trying to make up his mind. It is actually the *will* that makes the final and lasting decision. It is possible to have the intellectual conviction and the emotional feeling and still not be properly converted to Christ. Faith has legs. "Faith without works is dead." [16]

I heard about a man some years ago who was rolling a wheelbarrow back and forth across Niagara River on a tightrope. Thousands of people were shouting him on. He put a two-hundred-pound sack of dirt in the wheelbarrow and rolled it over, and then he rolled it back. Then he turned to the crowd and said, "How many of you believe that I can roll a man across?"

Everybody shouted! One man in the front row was very excited in his professed belief. The man pointed to this excited professor and said, "You're next!"

You couldn't see that man for dust! He actually didn't believe it. He said he believed it, he thought he believed it—but he was not willing to get in the wheelbarrow.

Just so with Christ. There are many people that say they believe on Him, they say they follow Him. But they never have gotten into the wheelbarrow. They actually never have committed and surrendered themselves wholly, one hundred per cent to Christ.

[16] *James* 2:20.

There are many people who ask, "Well, how much faith does it take?" Jesus said only the faith as of "a grain of mustard seed."

Others ask, "What kind of faith?" It is not a matter of any special kind of faith. There is only one kind, really. It is the *object* of the faith that counts. What is the object of your faith? The object of your faith must be Christ. Not faith in ritual, not faith in sacrifices, not faith in morals, not faith in yourself—not faith in anything but Christ!

Now the Bible teaches that faith will manifest itself in three ways. It will manifest itself in doctrine—in what you believe. It will manifest itself in worship—your communion with God and the fellowship of the church. It will manifest itself in morality—in the way you live and behave, which we will discuss in other chapters.

The Bible also teaches that faith does not end with trust in Christ for your salvation. Faith continues. Faith grows. It may be weak at first, but it will become stronger as you begin to read the Bible, pray, go to church, and experience God's faithfulness in your Christian life. After you have repented of sins and accepted Him by faith, then you must trust Him to keep you, strengthen you, enable you, sustain you. You will learn more and more how to rely on Christ for every need, in meeting every circumstance, and every trial. You will learn to say with Paul, "I am crucified with Christ; nevertheless I live; yet not I, but Christ liveth in me: and the life which I now live in the flesh I live by the faith of the Son of God, who loved me, and gave Himself for me." [17]

When you have saving faith in Jesus Christ, you have taken an additional step toward having peace with God.

[17] *Galatians 2:20.*

Chapter Eleven

THE NEW BIRTH

*Except a man be born again, he cannot see the king-
dom of God.*

JOHN 3:3.

IF I could come and have a heart-to-heart chat with you
in your living room, you probably would turn to me and
confess, "I am perplexed, confused, and mixed up. I have
transgressed God's laws. I have lived contrary to His
commandments. I thought I could get along without
God's help. I have tried to make up my own rules and
I've failed. The bitter lessons that I've learned have come
through suffering and tragic experience. What wouldn't
I give to be born again! What wouldn't I give to be able
to go back and start all over—what a different road I'd
travel if I could!"

If those words strike a familiar chord in your heart, if
they echo the thoughts that have been moving through
your mind, I want to tell you some glorious news. Jesus
said you can be born anew! You can have the fresh and
better start for which you've prayed. You can lose your
despised and sinful self and step forth a new person, a
clean and peaceful being from whom sin has been washed
away.

No matter how soiled your past, no matter how
snarled your present, no matter how hopeless your future
seems to be—there *is* a way out. There is a sure, safe,
everlasting way out—but there is only one! You have only
one choice to make. You have only one path to follow,

120

other than the torturous, unrewarding path you've been treading.

You can go on being miserable, discontented, frightened, unhappy, and disgusted with yourself and your life; or you can decide right now that you want to be born again. You can decide right now to wipe out your sinful past and make a new start, a fresh start, a right start. You can decide now to become the person that Jesus promised you could be.

The next logical question that you may ask is, "How can I have this rebirth? How can I be born again? How can I start afresh?"

This is the question that Nicodemus asked Jesus that night two thousand years ago under an Oriental sky. Being born again, however, means a great deal more than just a fresh start, or turning over a new leaf, or reforming. As we have already seen, the Bible teaches that you were born the first time into the physical world but your spiritual nature was born in sin. The Bible declares that you are "dead in trespasses and sins." [1]

The Bible teaches that there is nothing in your dead and sinful nature that can originate life. Being dead in sin, you cannot produce a life of righteousness. Many people are trying to produce a good, holy and righteous life without being born again, but they can do naught but fail. A corpse cannot generate life. The Bible teaches that "sin, when it is finished, bringeth forth death." [2] All of us are dead spiritually.

Your old nature cannot serve God. The Bible says, "The natural man receiveth not the things of the Spirit of God . . . neither can he know them." [3] In our natural state we are actually at enmity with God. We are not subject to the laws of God, neither indeed can we be, according to Romans 8:7.

The Bible also teaches that our old nature is totally corrupt. From its head to its feet "there is no soundness in it"; it is full of "wounds, and bruises, and putrifying

[1] *Ephesians 2:1.*   [2] *James 1:15.*
[3] *1 Corinthians 2:14.*

sores." [4] Its heart is deceitful above all things and desperately wicked. It is corrupt, according to deceitful lust.

The Bible also teaches that our old nature is a self-nature. It is incapable of being renovated. The Bible teaches that when we are born again, we put off the old man—we do not patch him up. The old self is to be crucified, not cultivated. Jesus said the cleansing of the outside of the cup and the platter leaves the inside just as foul as before.

The Bible also teaches that unless we have experienced this new birth we cannot get into the kingdom of heaven. Jesus even made it stronger. He said, "Ye *must* be born again." [5] There is nothing indefinite, nothing optional about that. He who would enter the kingdom of God must be born again.

Salvation is not just repairing the original self. It is a new self created of God in righteousness and true holiness. Regeneration is not even a change of nature, or a change of heart. Being born again is not a change—it is a regeneration, a new generation. It is a second birth. "Ye must be born again."

There is nothing about the old nature that God will accept. There is no soundness in it. The old nature is too weak to follow Christ. Paul said, "Ye cannot do the things that ye would." [6] They that are in the flesh cannot serve God. "Doth a fountain send forth at the same place sweet water and bitter? Can the fig tree, my brethren, bear olive berries?" asked James. [7]

The old man is described in Romans as "Their throat is an open sepulchre; with their tongues they have used deceit; the poison of asps is under their lips: Whose mouth is full of cursing and bitterness: Their feet are swift to shed blood: Destruction and misery are in their ways: . . . There is no fear of God before their eyes." [8]

How are you going to reform or patch up or change such throats and tongues and lips and feet and eyes as

[4] *Isaiah 1:6.*
[5] *John 3:7.*
[6] *Galatians 5:17.*
[7] *James 3:11,12.*
[8] *Romans 3:13-18.*

these? It is impossible. Jesus, knowing that it was impossible to change, patch up, and reform, said you must have a total new birth, "Ye must be born again." Jesus said, "That which is born of the flesh is flesh." On another occasion the Bible says, "Can the Ethiopian change his skin, or the leopard change his spots?" [9] Again in Romans the Bible says, "They that are in the flesh cannot please God." "In me (that is, my flesh) dwelleth no good thing." [10] Again the Bible says, "Without holiness no man shall see the Lord." [11]

The life that comes from the new birth cannot be obtained by natural development or self-effort. Man does not have by nature this holiness that God requires for heaven. In the new birth alone is the beginning of such a life to be found. In order to live the life of God we must have the nature of God.

The whole matter of receiving new life is like a coin. A coin has heads and tails. The receiving of new life has a divine side and a human side. We have seen the human side in our chapter on conversion, we have seen what you must do. Now let's see what God does.

Being born again is altogether a work of the Holy Spirit. There is nothing that you can do to obtain this new birth. The Bible says, "But as many as received Him, to them gave He power to become the sons of God, even to them that believed on His name: Which were born, not of blood, nor of the will of the flesh, nor of the will of man, but of God." [12] In other words, you cannot be born of blood; that means you cannot inherit the new birth.

You cannot inherit Christianity. You might have had a Christian father and mother, but that does not necessarily produce a Christian child. You could be born in a garage, but that doesn't make you an automobile.

You cannot be born of the will of the flesh, the Scripture says. In other words, there is nothing you can do about it. You are dead. A dead man has no life to do anything.

[9] *Jeremiah 13:23.*
[10] *Romans 7:18.*
[11] *Hebrews 12:14.*
[12] *John 1:12-13.*

Nor can you be born of the will of man. This new birth cannot be produced by human devices or schemes. Many people think they are automatically born again when they join a church or go through some religious ritual or make some New Year's resolution or give a large gift to an outstanding charitable institution. All of these are fine and right, but they do not produce the new birth.

Jesus told us we must *be* born again. The infinitive *to be* is passive. It shows that it is something that must be done for us. No man can "born" himself. He must *be* born. The new birth is wholly foreign to our will. In other words, the new birth is a divine work—we are born of God.

Nicodemus could not understand how he could be born the second time. In perplexity he asked twice, "How?"

Even though the new birth seems mysterious, that does not make it untrue. We may not understand the how of electricity, but we know that it lights our homes, runs our television and radio sets. We do not understand how the sheep grows wool, the cow grows hair, or the fowl grows feathers—but we know they do. We do not understand many mysteries, but we accept by faith the fact that at the moment we repent of sin and turn by faith to Jesus Christ we are born again.

It is the infusion of divine life into the human soul. It is the implantation or impartation of divine nature into the human soul whereby we become the children of God. We receive the breath of God. Christ through the Holy Spirit takes up residence in our hearts. We are attached to God for eternity. That means that if you have been born again you will live as long as God lives, because you are now sharing His very life.

When you are born again several results follow: First, it will increase your vision and *understanding*. The Bible says, "God, who commanded the light to shine out of darkness, hath shined in our hearts, to give the light of the knowledge of the glory of God in the face of Jesus Christ." [13] Again the Bible says, "The eyes of your un-

[13] *2 Corinthians 4:6.*

derstanding being enlightened." [14] Things that you used to laugh at as foolishness you now accept by faith. Your whole mental process is changed. God becomes the hub of your intellectual thinking. He becomes the center. The ego has been dethroned.

Second, your *heart* undergoes a revolution. The Bible says, "A new spirit will I put within you: and I will take away the stony heart out of your flesh, and I will give you an heart of flesh." [15] God says, "A new heart will I give you." [16]

Your affections have undergone a radical change. Your new nature loves God and the things that are pertaining to God. You love the finest and highest things in life. You reject the lower and baser. You have immediately a new appreciation for the social problems around you. Your heart beats with compassion for those who are less fortunate.

Third, your *will* undergoes a tremendous change. Your determinations are different. Your motives are changed. The Bible says, "Now the God of Peace . . . make you perfect in every good work to do His will, working in you that which is wellpleasing in His sight." [17]

This new nature that you receive from God is bent to the will of God. You will want to do only His will. You are utterly and completely devoted to Him. There is a new self-determination, inclination, disposition, a new principle of living, new choices. You seek to glorify God. You seek fellowship with other Christians in the church. You love the Bible. You love to spend time in prayer with God. Your whole disposition is changed. Whereas your life once was filled with unbelief, the root and foundation of all sin, and you once doubted God, you now believe Him, you now have utmost confidence and faith in God and His Word.

There may have been a time when pride was the very center of your life. You had ambitious thoughts of yourself, your powers, desires, and aims; but now that will

[14] *Ephesians 1:18.*   [15] *Ezekiel 36:26.*
[16] *Jeremiah 31:33.*   [17] *Hebrews 13:20,21.*

begin to change. There may have been a time when there was hatred in your life. Envy, discontent, and malice filled your thoughts toward others. That, too, will change.

There was a time when you could easily tell a lie. There were falsehoods and hypocrisies in many of your thoughts, words, and deeds. That is now all changed. There was a time when you gave in to the lust of the flesh. That is now changed. You have been born again. You may stumble into some of these traps that the Devil puts out for you, but immediately you will be sorry, confess your sins, and ask forgiveness, because you have been born again. Your very nature has changed.

There is an old story that tells about the pig and the lamb. The farmer brought the pig into the house. He gave him a bath, polished his hoofs, put some Chanel No. 5 on him, put a ribbon around his neck, and put him in the living room. The pig looked fine. He almost seemed to be acceptable to society and to friends that might come in, he was so fresh and clean. He made a very nice and companionable pet for a few minutes. But as soon as the door was opened, the pig left the living room and jumped into the first mud puddle that he could find. Why? Because he was still a pig at heart. His nature had not been changed. He had been changed outwardly but not inwardly.

Take a lamb, on the other hand. Put a lamb in a living room and then turn him out into the yard, and he will try his best to avoid all mud puddles. Why? Because his nature is that of a lamb.

You can take a man—dress him up, put him in the front row in church, and he almost looks like a saint. He may fool even his best friends for a while, but then put him in his office the next day, or put him at home or put him in the club on Saturday night, and you will see his true nature come out again. Why does he act that way? Because his nature has not changed. He has not been born again.

Now the moment you receive the new birth, the moment you are born again, the moment you receive this divine impartation of a new nature, you are justified in the sight of God. By being justified is meant "just-as-if-I'd" never sinned. Justification is that act of God whereby He declares an ungodly man to be perfect while he is still ungodly. God places you before Him as though you had never committed a sin.

As Paul says, "Who shall lay anything to the charge of God's elect? It is God that justifieth." [18] Your sins have been forgiven. God has buried them in the depths of the sea and placed them behind His back of forgetfulness. Every sin is completely wiped out. You stand before God as a debtor, and you have received your discharge, you have become reconciled to God. You were actually an enemy of God before. The Bible says, "And all things are of God, who hath reconciled us to Himself by Jesus Christ, and hath given to us the ministry of reconciliation." [19]

But more than all of that, you have been adopted into the family of God. You are now a child of God. "Having predestinated us unto the adoption of children by Jesus Christ to Himself, according to the good pleasure of His will." [20] You are now a member of the royal family of heaven. You have royal blood in your veins. You are a child of the King. There is a new sparkle in your eye. There is a spring in your step. There is a smile on your face. Even your friends notice the change that has taken place in your life. You have now been born again.

Certain changes will take place once you have been born again. First, there will be a different attitude toward sin. You will learn to hate sin as God hates it. You will detest it and abhor it.

Down in Houston, Texas, a man was born again in one of our meetings. He owned a liquor store. The next morning he had a sign on the front of his door saying, "Out of business."

I heard about a man some time ago who had been born again in an evangelistic service. He was known as the city drunk. He was called "Old John." Somebody

[18] *Romans 8:33.*   [19] *Romans 5:18.*
[20] *Ephesians 1:5.*

spoke to him the next morning on the street and said, "Good morning, Old John."

He said, "Who are you talking to? My name is not Old John. I'm *new* John." A complete revolution had taken place in his life.

Second, you will know that you have been born again because you will want to obey God. "And hereby we do know that we know Him, if we keep His commandments." [21]

Third, you will be separated from the world. The Bible says, "Love not the world, neither the things that are in the world. If any man love the world, the love of the Father is not in him." [22]

Fourth, there will be a new love in your heart for other people. The Bible says, "We know that we have passed from death unto life, because we love the brethren." [23]

Fifth, we will not practice sin. The Bible says, "We know that whosoever is born of God sinneth not." [24] We will not engage in sinful practices.

In Texas they tell a story about a man who used to hitch his horse every morning in front of the saloon. One morning the saloonkeeper came out and found that the horse was hitched in front of the Methodist Church. He saw the man walking down the street and called out, "Say, why is your horse hitched in front of the Methodist Church this morning?"

The man turned around and said, "Well, last night I was converted in the revival meeting, and I've changed hitching posts."

That's what it means to be born again. That's what it means to be converted. It means that you change hitching posts.

[21] *1 John 2:3.*   [22] *1 John 2:15.*
[23] *1 John 3:14.*   [24] *1 John 5:18.*

Chapter Twelve

HOW TO BE SURE

*These things have I written unto you that believe on
the name of the Son of God; that ye may know that
ye have eternal life, and that ye may believe on the
name of the Son of God.*

1 JOHN 5:13.

EVERY week I receive scores of letters from those who
say they have doubts and uncertainties concerning the
Christian life. Many come from genuine Christians who
seem to have none of the joy of Christian faith, or the
assurance, because they have failed to understand a basic
truth of Christian experience.

Now let's use this chapter to *sum up* what has happened to us. We have seen what it means to repent, to
have faith, and to be born again. Now, how can I be certain, how can I be sure that all of this has happened to
me? Many people with whom I talk have repented and
have believed and have been born again, but they often
lack the assurance of this conversion. Now let's go over
a few things that we've learned. First of all, becoming a
Christian can be a crisis experience in your life, or it can
be a process with a climactic moment of which you may
or may not be conscious.

Now do not misunderstand me, you do not become a
Christian as a result of a process of education. Some years
ago a great preacher said, "We must so educate and train
our youth in the Christian way of life that they will never
know when they were not Christians." Much of the
philosophy of religious education has been based upon
this premise, and perhaps many have missed the essence

of Christian experience because religious training took its place.

At the turn of the century, Professor Starbuck, a leading thinker in the field of psychology, observed that Christian workers generally were recruited from the ranks of those who had had a vital experience of conversion. He also observed that those who had a clear concept of what it means to be converted were mainly those who had come out of rural areas where in the early days they had had either little or no carefully planned religious training.

This is not a criticism of religious training, but it may be taken as a criticism of a false and improper use of religious training that becomes a substitute for the experience of the new birth.

To one of the most religious men of His times, Jesus said, "Except a man be born again, he cannot see the kingdom of God." [1] Nicodemus could not substitute his profound knowledge of religion for spiritual rebirth, and we have not progressed beyond this point in our generation.

The ugly larva in its cocoon spends much time in almost unnoticeable growth and change. But no matter how slow that growth may be, the moment comes when it passes through a crisis and emerges a beautiful butterfly. The weeks of silent growth are important, but they cannot take the place of that experience when the old and the ugly are left behind and the new and the beautiful come into being.

It is true that thousands of Christians do not know the exact day or hour that they came to know Christ. Their faith and life testify that consciously or unconsciously they have been converted to Christ. Whether they can remember it or not, there was a moment when they did cross over the line from death to life.

Probably everyone has had doubts and uncertainties at times in his religious experience. When Moses went up on Mount Sinai to receive the tables of the law from

[1] John 3:3.

the hand of God, he was lost for some time to the sight
of the Hebrews who stood anxiously waiting his return.
They finally became doubtful and said among themselves, "As for this Moses, the man that brought us up
out of the land of Egypt, we wot not what is become of
him." Their apostasy was a result of their doubting and
uncertainty.

This dreadful uncertainty that haunts the souls of multitudes grows out of misunderstanding of what constitutes
true religious experience. Many do not seem to understand the nature of Christian experience, while others
have been misinformed and are seeking something for
which we are not warranted by Scripture to expect.

More than three hundred times the word *faith* is mentioned in the New Testament with reference to man's
salvation, and many more times is it implied. The writer
of the Book of Hebrews said, "He that cometh to God
must believe that He is, and that He is a rewarder of
them that diligently seek Him." And again he said that
"Without faith it is impossible to please Him." [2]

It is because we have confused *faith* with *feeling* that
many experience the difficulty and uncertainty that is so
common among professing Christians today.

Faith always implies an object—that is, when we believe, we must believe something. That something I call
the *fact*. Let me give you, then, three words, three words
that must always be kept in the same order and never
rearranged. Let me give you these three words that will
point the way, for you, out of uncertainty to a confident
Christian life. These three words are *fact*, *faith*, and *feeling*. They come in this order and the order is essential.
If you confuse them, eliminate one, or add one, you will
end up in the mire of despair and continue to grope
about in semidarkness, without the joy and confidence of
one who can say, "I know Him in whom I have believed." [3]

If you are saved from sin at all, you are saved through
a personal faith in the Gospel of Christ as defined in the

[2] *Hebrews 11:6.*   [3] *2 Timothy 1:12.*

Scriptures. Though it may at first seem dogmatic and narrow to you, the fact remains that there is no other way. The Bible says, "I delivered unto you first of all that which I also received, how that Christ died for our sins according to the Scriptures; and that He was buried, and that He arose again the third day according to the Scriptures." [4] The Bible says that we are saved when our faith is in this objective fact. The work of Christ is a fact, His cross is a fact, His tomb is a fact, and His resurrection is a fact.

It is impossible to believe anything into existence. The Gospel did not come into being because men believed it. The tomb was not emptied of its deposit that first Easter because some faithful persons believed it. The fact always preceded the faith. We are psychologically incapable of believing without an object of our faith.

The Bible does not call upon you to believe something that is not credible, but to believe in the fact of history that in reality transcends all history. The Bible calls upon you to believe that this work of Christ, done for sin and for sinners, is effective in all who will risk their souls with Him. Trusting in Him for your eternal salvation is trusting in a fact.

Faith is second in this order of three words. Faith is rationally impossible where there is nothing to believe. Faith must have an object. The object of Christian faith is Christ. Faith means more than an intellectual assent to the claims of Christ. Faith involves the will. It is volitional. Faith demands action. If we actually believe, then we will live. Faith without works is dead. Faith actually means surrender and commitment to the claims of Christ. It means an acknowledgment of sin and a turning to Christ. We do not know Christ through the five physical senses, but we know Him through the sixth sense that God has given every man—which is the ability to believe.

Feeling is the last of the three words, and it must remain last in your thinking. I believe that much religious unrest and uncertainty is caused by earnest, honest seek-

[4] *1 Corinthians 15:3,4.*

ers after salvation who have a predetermined idea that they must be in some kind of an emotional state before they can experience conversion.

Those who are seeking salvation as it is presented through the Scriptures will want to know what kind of an experience the Bible leads you to expect. I speak to those who have gone often to an altar, or to an inquiry room, or perhaps have knelt beside a radio or television set when an invitation has been given to receive Christ. You have heard the message, you have known that you were a sinner in need of the Savior, you have recognized that your life is a spiritual wreck, you have tried every man-made scheme for self-improvement and for reformation but they all failed. In your lost and hopeless condition you looked to Christ for salvation. You believed that He could and would save you. You have often read His invitation to sinners when He said, "Come unto Me, all ye that labor and are heavy laden, and I will give you rest." [5] You have read the promise that says, "Him that cometh unto Me, I will in no wise cast out." You have read how He said, "If any man thirst, let him come unto Me and drink." [6]

In reading carefully through the New Testament to see just what kind of an experience you can expect, I find that the New Testament sets forth only one. There is just one experience for which you can look—only one feeling you can expect—and that is the experience of faith. Believing is an experience as real as any experience, yet many are looking for something more—some dramatic sensation that will bring a physical thrill, while others look for some spectacular manifestation. Many have been told to look for such sensations, but the Bible says that a man is "justified by faith" and not by feeling. A man is saved by trusting in the finished work of Christ on the cross and not saved by physical excitement or religious ecstasy.

But you may say to me, "What about feeling? Is there no place in saving faith for any feeling?" Certainly there

[5] *Matthew 11:28.*   [6] *John 7:37.*

is room for feeling in saving faith, but we are not saved by it. Whatever feeling there may be is only the result of saving faith, but it in itself is not what does the saving!

When I understand something of Christ's love for me as a sinner, I respond with a love for Christ—and love has feeling. But love for Christ is a love that is above the sensual accompaniments of human love. It is a love that is free from all self. The Bible says, "Perfect love casteth out fear." [7] And those who love Christ have that confidence in Him that raises them above all fear.

When I understand that Christ in His death gained a decisive victory over death and over sin, then I lose the fear of death. The Bible says that "He also Himself likewise took part of the same that through death He might destroy him that had the power of death, that is, the devil; And deliver them who through fear of death were all their lifetime subject to bondage." [8] Surely this also is a feeling. Fear is a kind of feeling, and to overcome fear with boldness and confidence in the very face of death is feeling and experience. But again I say, it is not the feeling of boldness and confidence that saves us, but it is our faith that saves us, and boldness and confidence result from our having trusted in Christ.

To have a guilty conscience is an experience. Psychologists may define it as a guilt complex, and may seek to rationalize away the sense of guilt; but once this has been awakened through the application of the law of God, no explanation will quiet the insistent voice of conscience. Many a criminal has finally given himself over to the authorities because the accusations of a guilty conscience were worse than prison bars.

The Bible teaches that Christ cleanses the conscience. The Bible says, "For if the blood of bulls and of goats and the ashes of an heifer sprinkling the unclean sanctifieth to the purifying of the flesh: How much more shall the blood of Christ, who through the eternal Spirit offered

[7] *1 John 4:18.*   [8] *Hebrews 2:14,15.*

Himself without spot to God, purge your conscience from dead works to serve the living God." [9]

To have a guilty conscience cleansed, and to be free from its constant accusation is an experience, but it is not the cleansing of the conscience that saves you; it is faith in Christ that saves, and a cleansed conscience is the result of having come into the right relationship with God.

Joy is a feeling. Inward peace is a feeling. Love for others is a feeling. Concern for the lost is a feeling.

Finally, someone may say, "I believe the historic facts of the gospel, but still I am not saved." Perhaps so, for the faith that saves has one distinguishing quality—saving faith is a faith that produces obedience, it is a faith that brings about a way of life. Some have quite successfully imitated this way of life for a time, but for those who trust Christ for salvation, that faith brings about in them a desire to live out that inward experience of faith. It is a power that results in godly living and surrender.

Let that intellectual faith, that historical faith that you may now have, yield itself to Christ in full surrender, earnestly desiring His salvation, and upon the authority of the Word of God you become a child of God. "But as many as received Him, to them gave He the right to become the sons of God, even to them that believe on His Name." [10]

[9] *Hebrews 9:13,14.*   [10] *John 1:12.*

PART THREE: THE RESULTS

Chapter Thirteen

ENEMIES OF THE CHRISTIAN

*For we wrestle not against flesh and blood, but
against principalities, against powers, against the
rulers of darkness of this world, against spiritual
wickedness in high places.*

EPHESIANS 6:12.

NOW that you have made your decision—now that you
have been born again—now that you have been converted—now that you have been justified—now that you
are a child of God—what next? Is that all there is to it?
Just one moment of decision and then it is all over? "Do
I have any more responsibilities," you ask?

Ah, yes, you have just begun the Christian life. You
have just been born into a new world—the spiritual
world. Everything is brand new. You are actually a spiritual baby. You need tenderness, love, care, nurture. You
need to be fed. You need protection. That is one of the
reasons why Christ established the church. You could not
possibly live the Christian life alone. You must have help
and fellowship.

Possibly you have already found that you have enemies. These are dangerous, vicious enemies that will use
any method to defeat you in your Christian life. Within
minutes after you made your decision you found these
enemies already at work: either you were tempted to
commit some sin, or you had a moment of depression and
discouragement. To be sure, everything is exciting and
thrilling just after you have made your decision for
Christ! But it is also natural to have doubts, problems,
questions, temptations, discouragements, and even difficulties.

The Bible teaches that you have three enemies that will be warring against you as long as you live. You must be prepared. They must be warded off.

First, let's look at these enemies whom we must face. Let's unmask them and see what they are, and who they are, and how they operate.

First—*the Devil*. We have already seen that the Devil is a mighty person who opposes God and tempts God's people. We have found that even though he was beaten at the cross by Christ he still has power to influence men for evil. The Bible calls him "the wicked one," [1] "the devil," [2] "a murderer," [3] "a liar, and the father of lies," [4] "an adversary" [5] who seeks to devour, "that old serpent" and "accuser of our brethren." [6]

The moment you made your decision for Christ he suffered a tremendous defeat. He is as mad as "hops" now. From now on he is going to tempt you and try to lead you into sin. Don't be alarmed. He cannot rob you of your salvation, and he need not rob you of your assurance and victory. He will do everything in his power to sow seeds of doubt in your mind as to whether your conversion is a reality or not. You cannot argue with him for he is the greatest debater of all time.

The moment of test has come with the first temptation. Remember to refuse any reliance upon your feelings; they will change like a weather vane in a whirlwind. His next approach probably will be to make you feel proud and important—to make you confident of your own powers, ambitions, desires, and aims. On another occasion he will put hatred in your heart. He will tempt you to say unkind and ungenerous things about others. He will put envy, discontent, and malice in your heart. Then on another occasion he will tempt you to lie, and you could easily find yourself being a hypocrite. Lying is one of the worst of all sins and can be committed by a thought, word, or deed. Anything that is intended to deceive an-

[1] *Matthew 13:19.*   [2] *Luke 4:33.*
[3] *John 8:44.*   [4] *John 8:44.*
[5] *1 Peter 5:8.*   [6] *Revelation 12:9-10.*

other person is lying. The Devil will do his best to make a liar of you. He also will try to get you to work for him to tempt others to sin—to try to lead other Christian friends astray. If you are not careful you will find yourself actually in the employ of the Devil. He is powerful, slick, crafty, wily, and subtle. He is called the "god of this world," [7] "the prince of this world," [8] "the prince and power of the air." [9]

You say "How can I overcome him? What can I do? Which way can I turn? Is there any escape?"

"There hath no temptation taken you but such as is common to man: but God is faithful, who will not suffer you to be tempted above that ye are able; but will with the temptation also make a way to escape, that ye may be able to bear it." [10]

God says in this verse that He has made a way of escape. Now remember this: temptation of the Devil is not a sign that your life is not right with God. It is actually a sign that you are right with God. Temptation is not sin. Also remember that God never tempts His own children. He never causes His children to doubt. All doubts and temptations come from the Devil. Remember also that Satan can only tempt. He can never compel you to yield to the temptation. Remember also that Satan has already been conquered by Christ. His power is made inoperative in the life of a fully trusting and yielded Christian who is completely dependent upon God.

Now the Bible says that we are to "resist the devil and he will flee" from us.[11] But before that, God says "Submit yourselves . . . to God." If you have fully submitted, one hundred per cent yielded and surrendered yourself to Christ, then you can "resist the devil," and the Bible promises he will flee from you. The Devil will tremble when you pray. He will be defeated when you quote or read a passage of Scripture to him, and will run like a scalded dog when you resist him. You can keep the Devil

[7] *2 Corinthians 4:4.*
[8] *John 12:31.*
[9] *Ephesians 2:2.*
[10] *1 Corinthians 10:13.*
[11] *James 4:7.*

on the run twenty-four hours a day in the power of Christ.

Your second enemy is *the world*. The *world* means the cosmos, this world system. The world has a tendency to lead us into sin—evil companions, pleasures, fashions, opinions, and aims of the world.

You will find in your born-again experience that your pleasures have been lifted into an entirely new and glorious realm. Many non-Christians have accused the Christian life as being a set of rules, taboos, vetoes, and prohibitions. This is another lie of the Devil. It is not a series of "don'ts," but a series of "dos." You become so busy in the work of Christ and so completely satisfied with the things of Christ that you do not have time for the things of the world.

Suppose someone should offer me a plateful of crumbs after I had eaten a T-bone steak. I would say "No, thank you, I am already satisfied."

Young Christian, that is the secret. You are so filled with the things of Christ, so enamored of the things of God, that you do not have time for sinful pleasures of this world.

Worldliness, however, has been vastly misunderstood on the part of thousands of Christians. It needs a little clarification. It is probably one of the greatest difficulties that meets a young and inexperienced Christian.

Dr. Griffith Thomas has said, "There are certain elements of daily life which are not sinful in themselves, but which have a tendency to lead to sin if they are abused. Abuse literally means extreme use, and in many instances overuse of things lawful becomes sin. Pleasure is lawful in use but unlawful in its overuse. Ambition is an essential part of true character, but it must be fixed on lawful objects and exercised in proper proportion. Our daily occupation, reading, dress, friendships and other similar phases of life are all legitimate and necessary, but can easily become illegitimate, unnecessary and harmful. Thought about the necessities of life is absolutely essential, but this can easily degenerate into anxiety, and then as Christ reminds us in the parable, the cares of this life choke the spiritual seed in the heart. Making of money is necessary for daily living, but money-making is apt to degenerate into money-loving and then the deceitfulness of riches enters into and spoils our spiritual life. Worldliness is thus not confined to any particular rank, walk, or circumstance of life so that we cannot separate this class from that and call one worldly and the other unworldly . . . One spiritual and the other unspiritual. Worldliness is a spirit, an atmosphere, an influence permeating the whole of life and human society, and it needs to be guarded against constantly and strenuously."

The Bible says "Love not the world, neither the things that are in the world." [12] The Bible also warns that the world and the "lust thereof" shall pass away, "but he that doeth the will of God" shall abide forever.[13]

However, under certain conditions these can become perplexing problems in our modern-day living. Many young people come and ask me, "Is this wrong?" or "Is that wrong?" "Is this sinful?" or "Is that sinful?" One simple question, earnestly and prayerfully asked, will settle about ninety per cent of your problems along this line. Just ask this question to yourself every time, "What would Christ have me to do?" Another question you can ask is, "Can I ask His blessing upon this particular thing for me?" "What would Christ think about my amusements, recreation, books, companions, and television programs?" We cannot compromise or bargain here. There must be an out-and-out stand for Christ.

It does not mean that in society we are snobs or have a superiority complex, lest we be in danger of spiritual pride—which would be far worse than any worldliness. But today there are so many professing Christians who are walking hand in hand with the world that you cannot tell the difference between the Christian and the sinner. This should never be.

The Christian should stand out like a sparkling diamond against a rough background. He should be more wholesome than anyone else. He should be poised, cul-

[12] 1 John 2:15.   [13] 1 John 2:17.

tured, courteous, gracious, but firm in the things that he does and does not do. He should laugh and be radiant, but he should refuse to allow the world to pull him down to its level.

The Bible says that "whatsoever it not of faith is sin," [14] and the Bible again says that he that doubteth is condemned if he does it. In other words, we are never to do anything of which we are not perfectly clear and certain. If you have a doubt about that particular thing that is bothering you, as to whether it is worldly or not, the best policy is "don't do it."

The third enemy that you will face immediately is *the lust of the flesh*. The flesh is that evil tendency of your inward self. Even after you are converted, sometimes your old, sinful cravings will return. You become startled and wonder where they come from. The Bible teaches that the old nature, with all its corruption, is still there and that these evil temptations come from nowhere else. In other words, "a traitor is living within." "That wretched bent toward sin is ever present to drag you down." War has been declared! You now have two natures in conflict, and each one is striving for the victory.

The Bible teaches "the flesh lusteth against the Spirit, and the Spirit against the flesh." [15] It is the battle of the self-life and the Christ-life. This old nature cannot please God. It cannot be converted, or even patched up. Thank God, when Jesus died He took you with Him, and the old nature can be made inoperative and you can "reckon ye also yourselves to be dead indeed unto sin." [16] This is done by faith.

However, you must distinguish very carefully again between use and abuse—between that which is lawful and that which is unlawful. Some of these things that will be cropping up may be sinful lusts, or they may not be.

As Dr. Thomas says, "The original meaning of the word lust is 'strong desire' and not necessarily a sinful desire, since there are certain desires of our physical nature—

[14] *Romans 14:23.*   [15] *Galatians 5:17.*
[16] *Romans 6:11.*

such as hunger and thirst—which we have in common with the animal world and which, in themselves, are natural and not sinful. It is only their abuse that is evil. Hunger is a natural lust. Gluttony is a sinful lust. Thirst is a natural lust. Intemperance is a sinful lust. Sloth is a sinful lust. Marriage is according to the will of God and the dictates of human nature, physical, mental and social. Adultery is a sin and is opposed to the will of God and to all that is pure in body, mind and heart. But there are other lusts of the flesh which are sensually and inherently sinful. Such as, for instance, the desire to gratify at all cost our hatred and revenge. We must, therefore, distinguish carefully between the lust which is simply a strong desire, and the same lust as a sinful desire. Sins of the flesh are in some respects the most terrible of all because they represent the yearnings of the nature to do evil. Neither the Devil nor the world, nor even our own evil heart can compel us to sin. It must be by our consent and will and it is at this point that our evil nature comes in with its awful power and possibility of evil."

Paul said he had no confidence in the flesh. On another occasion he said, "I make no provision for the flesh." [17] On another occasion he said, "I keep my body under." [18] We are so to completely yield and surrender ourselves to God that we can, by faith, reckon the old nature dead indeed unto sin.

These then, are our three foes: the Devil, the world, and the flesh. Our attitude toward them as Christians can be summed up in one word—*renounce*. There can be no bargaining, compromise, or hesitation. Absolute renunciation is the only possible course to a Christian seeking complete victory. In relation to the Devil, we resist him only as we submit ourselves to God. In relation to the world, the Bible says, "This is the victory that overcometh the world, even our faith." [19] In relation to the flesh, the Bible says, "Walk in the Spirit, and ye shall not fulfill the lust of the flesh." [20]

---

[17] *Romans 13:14.*
[18] *1 Corinthians 9:27.*
[19] *1 John 5:4.*
[20] *Galatians 5:16.*

Here is glorious news to you who have already been fighting these battles and temptations. You are not asked to fight the battle alone. The Bible says in Romans 8:13 that you, *by the Spirit*, shall put to death the deeds of the body. Remember, Jesus promised that He would never leave us, or forsake us. Remember Jesus promised us that after He left the earth He would send Another—the Third Person of the Trinity—the Holy Spirit, who is called a Comforter (which actually means "one that helps alongside") that He may abide with us forever.[21] Jesus said, "I am not going to leave you alone. I will come to you. I will come to you in the person of the Holy Spirit."

The Holy Spirit is the most powerful Being in the world today. The time of the Old Testament was an age of God the Father. During the time that Jesus was on earth it was an age of God the Son. Now we are living, since Pentecost, in the age of God the Holy Spirit.

The Bible says that the moment you accepted Christ as Savior the Holy Spirit took up residence in your heart. Your body is now "the temple of the Holy Ghost *which is in you.*" [22] Paul even warned that if any man hath not the Spirit of Christ he is none of His.

You say, "But I don't feel anything down in my heart. I don't feel the Spirit of God in me."

Disregard feelings. You're not saved by feeling, and you may or may not feel the Spirit. Accept Him by faith as a fact. He lives within you right now to help you live the Christian life. He is living in you in order to magnify, glorify, and exalt Christ in you so that you can live a happy, victorious, radiant, Christ-honoring life.

The Bible commands "Be filled with the Spirit." [23] If you are filled with the Spirit, then you are going to produce the fruit of the Spirit, which is "love, joy, peace, longsuffering, gentleness, goodness, faith, meekness, temperance." [24] To be filled with the Spirit is not optional. It is a command to be obeyed—a duty to be done.

How do you know that you are filled? And how can

[21] *John 14:16.*   [22] *1 Corinthians 6:19.*
[23] *Ephesians 5:18.*   [24] *Galatians 5:22-23.*

you be filled? Is it some emotional experience through which you must pass? No. When you are fully cleansed of every known sin and completely yielded and surrendered to Christ, then you can accept by faith that you are filled with the Spirit of God. That means that He can have *all* of you. There is nothing else in your heart except Him. Consecration actually is surrender—total, absolute, unconditional, irreversible surrender. "I beseech you, therefore, brethren, by the mercies of God, that ye present your bodies a living sacrifice, holy, acceptable unto God, which is your reasonable service." [25]

It is only the consecrated, Spirit-filled Christian who can have victory over the world, the flesh, and the Devil. It is the Holy Spirit who will do the fighting for you. "We wrestle not against flesh and blood, but against principalities, against powers, against the rulers of darkness." [26] This is spiritual warfare. You cannot fight against these three enemies with normal weapons. Only as we become channels and let the Holy Spirit do the fighting through us are we going to get complete victory. Don't hold back anything from Christ. Let Him be completely the Lord and Master of your life. He said, "Ye call me Master and Lord: and ye say well; for so I am." [27]

A little child playing one day with a very valuable vase put his hand into it and could not withdraw it. His father, too, tried his best, but all in vain. They were thinking of breaking the vase when the father said, "Now, my son, make one more try. Open your hand and hold your fingers out straight as you see me doing, and then pull."

To their astonishment the little fellow said, "Oh, no, father. I couldn't put my fingers out like that, because if I did I would drop my penny."

Smile, if you will—but thousands of us are like that little boy, so busy holding on to the world's worthless penny that we cannot accept liberation. I beg you to drop the little copper in your heart. Surrender! Let go, and let God have His way in your life.

[25] *Romans 12:1.* [26] *Ephesians 6:12.*
[27] *John 13:13.*

Now, after you have given yourself completely to Christ in consecration, remember that God has accepted what you have presented. Here we exercise faith again. "Him that cometh unto Me I will in no wise cast out." You have come to Him; now He has received you. As a result of a fully yielded, consecrated, Spirit-filled life you will have courage and boldness that you have never known before.

The Spirit-filled man knows only the fear of God, but he has no other fear. All other fears will immediately leave. He will have supernatural courage and boldness to take his stand for Christ. If you go through the Book of Acts you will find the word *boldness* used many times by the Spirit-filled apostles.

Not only will you have boldness, but you will produce the fruit of the Spirit. Now remember that these fruits of the Spirit are *of the Spirit*. You cannot produce them yourself. They are supernatural fruit that will characterize your life from day to day and they must be supernaturally produced. There will be love. The great commandment that Jesus left us was that "ye love one another as I have loved you." [28] You will love your fellow man with a supernatural love, regardless of race, creed, or political affiliation. Bitterness, strife, and envy will cease and brotherly love will prevail.

There will be joy. One of the characteristics of the Christian is inward joy. No matter what the circumstances, there will be a joyful heart and a radiant face. So many Christians go around with droopy faces that give no outshining glory to God. Upon meeting a Christian it is easy to tell whether or not he is a victorious, spiritual, yielded Christian. A true Christian should be relaxed and radiant, capable of illuminating and not depressing his surroundings. The Bible says, "For the joy of the Lord is your strength." [29]

There will be peace. Paul said, "Troubled on every side, yet not distressed; we are perplexed, but not in despair; persecuted, but not forsaken; cast down, but not

[28] *John 15:12.*   [29] *Nehemiah 8:10.*

destroyed." [30] We could go through all the rest of the supernatural list—long-suffering, gentleness, goodness, faith, meekness, and temperance and see how all of this fruit flourishes in the lives of those who are truly yielded and Spirit-filled.

The victory is yours. Claim it! It is your birthright. You have no reason ever to suffer even one defeat. You can live "high, wide and handsome." The best is yours. Life can be one grand, glorious exciting adventure. You will want to live every minute of it so much that you may regret having to go to bed at night—and you will certainly welcome getting up each morning to live another day for Christ. For every day will be wonderful and thrilling—filled with opportunities to be of service, filled with moments to spend with God, filled with the knowledge that you are safe forevermore with Jesus!

[30] *2 Corinthians 4:8-9.*

Chapter Fourteen

RULES OF THE CHRISTIAN LIFE

*And as ye would that men should do to you, do ye
also to them likewise.*

LUKE 6:31.

WHETHER you are playing a game, driving a car, or
baking a cake, there are certain rules that must be followed if you are to succeed.

The Bible teaches that the Christian life is one of constant growth. When you are born again, you are born into
the spiritual world. You become a baby in God's family.
It is God's purpose that you will grow into full stature
and become mature in Christ. It would be against the
law of God and nature if you were to remain a baby and
thus become a spiritual dwarf. In 2 Peter 3:18, the Bible
says that we are to grow. This implies steady development, constant enlargement, increasing wisdom.

In order to grow properly certain rules must be observed for good spiritual health. First: you should *read
your Bible daily.* Your spiritual life needs food. What
kind of food? Spiritual food. Where do you find this
spiritual food? In the Bible, the Word of God. The Bible
reveals Christ, who is the Bread of Life for your hungry
soul, and the water of life for your thirsty heart. If you
fail to partake of daily spiritual nourishment, you will
starve and lose your spiritual vitality. The Bible says,
"Desire the sincere milk of the Word, that ye may grow
thereby." [1] Read it, study it, meditate on it, memorize it.

[1] *1 Peter 2:2.*

Ninety-five per cent of the difficulties you will experience as a Christian can be traced to a lack of Bible study and reading.

Do not be content to skim through a chapter merely to satisfy your conscience. Hide the Word of God in your heart. A little portion well digested is of greater spiritual value to your soul than a lengthy portion scanned hurriedly. Do not be discouraged because you cannot understand it all. Read simple portions of the Bible first. You do not feed a baby beefsteak the first day—you give it milk.

I would suggest that you start by reading the Gospel of John. As you read, the Holy Spirit will enlighten the passages for you. He will illuminate the difficult words and make obscure meanings clear. Even though you cannot remember all you have read, or understand it all, *go on reading*. The very practice of reading in itself will have a purifying effect upon your mind and heart. Let nothing take the place of this daily exercise.

Second: *learn the secret of prayer*. You now have a Heavenly Father. He hears and answers prayer. Jesus said, "Ask anything in My name and I will do it." [2] Again He said, "All things whatsoever ye shall ask in prayer believing ye shall receive." [3] Every man whose life has counted for the church or for the kingdom of God has been a man of prayer. You cannot afford to be too busy to pray. A prayerless Christian is a powerless Christian. Christ spent hours in prayer. He sometimes spent the night on a mountain top in solitary communion with God the Father. If He had to pray, how much more do we need to pray!

Your prayers may falter at first. You may be awkward and inarticulate. But the Holy Spirit who lives within you will help you and teach you. Every prayer that you pray will be answered. Sometimes the answer may be "No," and sometimes it is "Wait," but nevertheless it will be answered.

Your petitions should always be conditioned by "Thy

[2] *John 14:14.*   [3] *Matthew 21:22.*

will be done." "Delight thyself also in the Lord and He shall give thee the desires of thine heart." [4] But the delighting of oneself in Him precedes the fulfillment of our desires. God will always do what is best for His children.

Remember that you can pray any time, anywhere. Washing dishes, digging ditches, working in the office, in the shop, on the athletic field—you can pray and God will answer!

Have a systematic method of prayer. Prayer combined with Bible study makes for a complete and glorious Christian life. The Bible says, "Pray without ceasing." [5] If you have special prayer periods that you set aside during the day, your unconscious life will be saturated with prayer between the prayer periods. It is not enough for you to get out of bed in the morning and just bow your knee and repeat a few sentences. There should be stated periods in which you slip apart with God.

The Devil will fight you every step of the way. He will cause the baby to cry, the telephone to ring, someone to knock at the door—there will be many interruptions, but keep at it! Don't be discouraged. Soon you will find that these periods of prayer are the greatest delight of your life. You will look forward to them with more anticipation than to anything else. Without constant, daily, systematic prayer your life will seem barren, discouraging, and fruitless. Without constant prayer you never can know that inner peace that God wants to give you.

Third: *rely constantly on the Holy Spirit*. Remember that Christ dwells in you through the Holy Spirit. Your body is now the dwelling place of the Third Person of the Trinity. Do not ask Him to help you as you would a servant. Ask Him to come in and do it *all*. Ask Him to take over in your life. Tell Him how weak, helpless, unstable, and unreliable you are. Stand aside and let Him take over in all the choices and decisions of your life.

It is impossible for you to hold out in your Christian life—but He can hold you. It is very difficult for Him to hold you if you are struggling, fighting, and striving.

[4] *Psalm 37:4.*   [5] *1 Thessalonians 5:17.*

Just relax and rest in the Lord. Let go all those inner tensions and complexes. Rely completely on Him. Do not fret and worry about important decisions—let Him make them for you. Do not worry about tomorrow—He is the God of tomorrow, He sees the end from the beginning. Do not worry about the necessities of life—He is there to supply and provide. A true victorious Christian will be free from worries, inner conflicts, and tensions. In perfect reliance on the Holy Spirit, you will find that many of your physical and mental ailments will disappear.

Fourth: *attend church regularly*. John Wesley once said, "The Bible knows nothing of solitary religion." Christianity is a religion of fellowship. Following Christ means love, righteousness, service; and these can only be achieved and expressed through social relations. These social relationships are to be found in the church.

The church is Christ's organization upon earth. It is a place where we worship God, learn His Word, and fellowship with other Christians. The Bible calls the church "a holy nation," "God's own people," "the household of God," "a holy temple in the Lord," "a dwelling place of God in the Spirit," "the body of Christ." These are all figures of speech, symbols, or pictures used to indicate the spiritual reality of the church.

Nothing can take the place of church attendance. If you are a true follower of Christ you will scorn such flimsy excuses as the weather being too hot or too cold, rain or snow, as unworthy of a true follower of Christ. There are many people who say that they can stay at home on Sunday morning and worship God in their own minds. The person who does only this fails to give God the complete worship to which He has a right, for God is the Creator of our bodies, no less than of our minds and souls; therefore both the mind and the body should participate in rendering to God a complete act of worship.

There are many who say they can stay at home and listen to a sermon on the radio and that that takes the place of church service. That is not enough. You do not go to church to hear a sermon. You go to church to worship God and to serve Him in the fellowship of other

Christians. You cannot be a successful and happy Christian without being faithful in church. In the church you will find your place of service. We are saved to serve. The happy Christian is the busy Christian.

Fifth: *be a witnessing Christian*. If you are faithfully practicing the four preceding rules this one will take care of itself—just as it follows naturally that if a cup is being filled continually it is bound to overflow.

You are now a duly appointed and commissioned ambassador of the King of Kings. You are to let your flag fly high over your embassy. Suppose our ambassador to Russia should order the American flag pulled down because it is not popular in Russia—we would soon call him home! He would not deserve to represent the United States.

If you are not willing to let your flag fly in the home, in the office, in the shop, on the campus—then you are not worthy to be an ambassador for Christ! You are to take your stand and let all those round about you know that you are a Christian. You are to bear witness for Christ.

We witness in two ways: by life and by word—neither by itself is enough. God's purpose for you and me after we have been converted is that we be witnesses to His saving grace and power. You are to be a commando for Christ. You are to be a minuteman for Him.

Christ said, "Whoever therefore shall confess me before men, him will I confess also before my Father which is in heaven." [6] Acts 28:23 presents a thrilling scene. Paul, held in bonds at Rome, persuaded men concerning Jesus, from morning to evening. Concerning each of us it should be said every day, "Behold a sower went forth to sow."

Very little originality is permitted a Western Union messenger boy. His sole obligation is to carry the message he receives from the office to the person to whom it is addressed. He may not like to carry that message. It may contain bad news or distressing news for the person to whom he carries it. He cannot stop on the way, open the

[6] *Matthew 10:32.*

envelope, and change the wording of the telegram. His duty is to take the message.

We young Christians have the Word of God. Our Great Commander has said, "Go, and take this message to a dying world." Some are neglecting it. Some are tearing up the message and substituting one of their own. Some are taking out a part of it. Some are telling the people that the Lord does not mean what He says. Others are saying that He really did not write the message but that it was written by ordinary men who are mistaken about the meaning of it.

Let us remember that the Apostle Paul exhorted the Christian centuries ago to teach only the Word. Remember we are sowing seed. Some indeed may fall on beaten paths and some among thorns, but it is our business to keep on sowing. We are not to stop sowing because some of the soil looks unpromising.

We are holding a light. We are to let it shine! Though it may seem but a twinkling candle in a world of blackness, it is our business to let it shine.

We are blowing a trumpet. In the din and noise of battle the sound of our little trumpet may seem to be lost, but we must keep sounding the alarm to those who are in danger.

We are kindling a fire. In this cold world full of hatred and selfishness our little blaze may seem to be unavailing, but we must keep our fire burning.

We are striking with a hammer. The blows may seem only to jar our hands as we strike, but we are to keep on hammering.

We are using a sword. The first or second thrust of our sword may be evaded and all of our efforts at striking deep into the enemy may seem hopeless, but we are to keep wielding our sword—it is the "sword of the Spirit."

We have bread for a hungry world. The people may seem to be so busy feeding on other things that they will not accept the Bread of Life, but we must keep on giving it, offering it to the souls of men.

We have water for famishing people. We must keep

standing and crying out, "Ho, every one that thirsteth, come ye to the waters."

We must persevere. We must never give up. Keep using the Word!

Jesus said that much of your seed will find good soil and spring up and bear fruit. The fire in your heart and on your lips will kindle a sacred flame in some cold hearts and woo them to Christ. The hammer will break some hard hearts and make them contrite and yield to God. The sword will pierce the armor of sin and cut away the self-satisfaction and the pride, and open hearts to the Spirit of God. Some hungry men and women will take the Bread of Life, and some famishing souls will find the water of life.

Be a soul winner! The most thrilling experience known to man is to win another to Jesus Christ. It has been my privilege to win thousands to a saving knowledge of Christ. I never cease to thrill at seeing a man put his hand out and say, "I accept your Christ." This is worth more than all the money in all the world. There is no happiness, no experience, no romantic adventure comparable to the thrill of winning another person to Christ. Be a soul winner! Be a witness!

The Bible says, "He that winneth souls is wise." [7] "And they that be wise shall shine as the brightness of the firmament; and they that turn many to righteousness as the stars for ever and ever." [8]

"Ye are the salt of the earth." [9] Salt makes one thirsty. Does your life makes others thirsty for the water of life?

Sixth: *let love be the ruling principle of your life.* Jesus said to those who followed Him, "By this shall all men know that ye are My disciples, if ye have love one to another." In another part of the Bible we find the same thing stated by John, "Beloved, let us love one another, for love is of God; and every one that loveth is born of God, and knoweth God. He that loveth not knoweth not God, for God is love. In this was manifested the love of

[7] *Proverbs 11:30.*   [8] *Daniel 12:3.*
[9] *Matthew 5:13.*

God toward us, because that God sent His only begotten Son into the world, that we might live through Him. Herein is love, not that we loved God, but that He loved us, and sent His Son to be the propitiation for our sins." [10]

Of all the gifts God offers His children, love is the greatest. Of all the fruits of the Holy Spirit, love is the first.

The Bible declares that we who follow Christ should be just as much in love with each other as God was in love with us when He sent His Son to die on the cross. The Bible says that the moment we come to Christ He gives us supernatural love, and that that love is shed abroad in our hearts by the Holy Spirit. The greatest demonstration of the fact that we are Christians is that we love one another. If you learn this secret of God early in your Christian experience, you will have gone a long way toward a mature, happy Christian life.

Seventh: *be an obedient Christian.* Let Christ have first place in all the choices of your life. Make Him Lord and Master. Let Him pilot your ship.

Eighth: *learn how to meet temptation.* As we have already learned, temptation is natural. Temptation is not sin. It is *yielding* that is sin. God never brings temptation to you. He allows it to test you. It is the work of the Devil. Recognize it as such. One way to meet temptation is to quote a verse of Scripture at the Tempter—he will always run, for he cannot stand the Word of God.

When Jesus was tempted in the wilderness, the only resource that He had was the Word of God. He said three times, "It is written."

You say to the Devil, "Thus saith the Lord," and he will flee. At the same time let Christ through the Holy Spirit do the fighting for you. Like the little girl—she said, "Every time I hear the Devil knock, I send Jesus to the door."

Everyone has temptations but some folks entertain them. They seem to enjoy being tempted. Chase a mouse with a broom and you will notice that he isn't eying the

[10] *1 John 4:7-10.*

broom. He is looking for a hole. Get your eyes off the temptation and onto Christ!

I once asked an army officer which he would rather have on the field of battle—courage or obedience. He flashed right back, "Obedience!"

God would rather have your obedience than anything else. In order to be obedient you must know His commands. That is another reason for the necessity of studying and reading the Bible. The Bible is your compass and rule book. Obey what God tells you.

Ninth: *be a wholesome Christian.*

It has been well said that "Some Christians are so heavenly minded they are no earthly good."

Certainly the Bible teaches separation from sin, but the Bible says nowhere that we are to be unwholesomely peculiar and unnatural. You are to be radiant. You should be chivalrous, courteous, clean of body, pure of mind, poised, and gracious. Silly flirtations, unhealthy gossip, shady conversations, suggestive amusements should be avoided like rattlesnakes. Your appearance should be neat, clean, attractive, and as much as possible in style, with good taste. Extremes should be avoided in all directions. You should strive to be the ideal gentleman or the ideal lady. Your life and appearance should commend the Gospel and make it attractive to others. As Dr. Barnhouse has adequately said, "Men may not read the gospel in sealskin, or the gospel in morocco, or the gospel in cloth covers; but they can't get away from the gospel in shoe leather."

Tenth: *live above your circumstances.* God made you as you are! He placed you where you are! So you can best serve and glorify Him just as you are, where you are. Some people are always looking on the other side of the fence because they think the grass is greener. They spend so much time wishing things were different, and thinking up alibis for why they are not, that they overlook all the advantages and opportunities that are open to them right where they are.

Be as the Apostle Paul when he said, "But none of

these things move me." [11] Paul said he had learned how to abound and how to be abased. He had learned to be every inch a Christian even in prison. Don't let your circumstances get you down. Learn to live comfortably and graciously within them.

These rules and suggestions may seem simple—but keep them—they work. I have seen them tested in the lives of thousands. I have tested them in my own life. Properly and faithfully kept, they will give you peace of soul, happiness, peace of mind, and pleasure, and you will have learned the secret of living life with satisfaction.

[11] *Acts 20:24.*

Chapter Fifteen

THE CHRISTIAN
AND THE CHURCH

In whom ye also are builded together for an habitation of God through the Spirit.

EPHESIANS 2:22.

MAN is a social animal, gregarious by nature, and finds his greatest sense of security and satisfaction in the company of others who share his interests and attitudes. Of all the many groups into which humans have collected themselves, of all the many tribes, clans, organizations, and societies throughout history, none has been so powerful, so far-reaching, or more universal than the church.

In primitive times, men gathered together for mutual protection, and at a far later date they learned to join together for mutual benefit and pleasure. With more advanced civilization, secret societies came into being, to give their members a sense of being "set apart" and therefore distinguished from nonmembers. Special oaths, rituals, and codes were established and given great significance.

Racial and national groups were established with membership restricted to those of similar place of origin, or with allegiance to a common flag. Country clubs, college fraternities, lodges, literary societies, political parties, military organizations—all of these, from the most select "gentlemen's club" to the high school "gang," represent man's need to find comfort and reassurance in the company of others who approve of his way of life, because their own way of life is similar.

Nowhere, however, has man found this comfort, this reassurance, this peace to the extent that he has found it in the church, for all other groups are obviously man-inspired. They draw artificial boundaries and set up only the illusion of protection; while the church provides a living, vibrant organism that draws its power from within itself, instead of relying upon outside sources to give it meaning and vitality.

The word *church* is an English translation of the Greek word *ecclesia,* which means "the called-out ones," or an assembly of people. Although *church* soon became a distinctively Christian word, it has a pre-Christian history. Throughout the Greek world the word *church* was the designation of the regular assembly of the whole body of citizens in a free city-state. A group of the citizens would be called out by the herald for the discussion and decision of public business. This same word *church* was also used in the Old Testament and is translated in English as "congregation" or "community" of Israel in which members were designated as the called-out people of God. Thus we find Stephen in the Book of Acts using it when he describes Moses as "he that was in the church in the wilderness." In the first century, therefore, the word *church* would suggest to the Greek a self-governing, democratic society; to the Jew, a theocratic society whose members were the subjects of God.

The word *church* as applied to the Christian society was first used by Jesus Himself when He told Peter, "Upon this rock I will build my church, and the gates of hell shall not prevail against it." [1] Thus Jesus Christ Himself founded the church. He is the great cornerstone upon which the church is built. He is the foundation of all Christian experience, and the church is founded upon Him. "For other foundation can no man lay than that is laid, which is Jesus Christ." [2] Jesus proclaimed Himself to be the founder of the church, the builder of the church, and the church belongs to Him and to Him alone. He has promised to live with, and in, all those who

---

[1] *Matthew 16:18.*   [2] *1 Corinthians 3:11.*

are members of His church. Here is not only an organization but an organism which is completely unlike anything else that the world has ever known: God Himself living with, and in, ordinary men and women who are members of His church.

The New Testament teaches that while there is actually only one church there can be any number of local churches formed into various denominations and societies or councils. These local churches and denominational groups may be divided along national and theological lines, or according to the temperament of their members. However, the New Testament teaches that even though there may be many cleavages and divisions within the structure of the church, yet we have only "one Lord." As the hymn puts it, "The church's one foundation is Jesus Christ her Lord."

Jesus Christ is the head of this great universal church. From Him must spring all the activities and teachings of the church, for He is the fountainhead of all Christian religious experience.

In this day of electronics it is easy to draw a comparison with a far-flung telephone system in which there is one central station toward which all wires converge and from which all connections are made. In a railroad system there is always one central office from which orders governing the operations of all trains originate. In the army, one commanding general issues orders to the many groups under his jurisdiction. His various subordinates may interpret his orders in slightly different ways, but his orders still remain the basis for their conduct.

In relation to the church, Jesus Christ stands in the position of the commanding general. It is upon His orders that the church has its existence, its very power comes directly from Him, and it is up to every church group to follow His commands as closely as possible. Just as the commanding general expects to have his orders carried out faithfully, so does Jesus expect every branch of the church to abide by His teachings to the fullest.

The church has been widely criticized for many intramural squabbles, much hair-splitting and apparent lack of unity. These, however, are superficial things; these are the conflicts that come from the slightly varying interpretations of the general's orders and in no way reflect upon the wisdom of the general or his absolute authority in issuing his orders!

Study the underlying beliefs of the various denominations and you will find that basically and historically they are almost identical. They may differ widely in ritual, they may seem to lock horns over theological technicalities; but fundamentally they all recognize Jesus Christ as God incarnate, who died upon the cross and rose again that man might have salvation—and that is the all-important fact to all humanity.

Now that you have accepted Christ as your Savior and put your trust and confidence in Him, you have already become a member of the great universal church. You are a member of the household of faith. You are a part of the body of Christ. Now you are called upon to obey Christ, and if you obey Christ, you will follow His example of joining with others in the worship of God. "Not forsaking the assembling of ourselves together, as the manner of some is." [8]

It has been said, "In practical terms this membership of the body of Christ must actually mean membership of some local manifestation of His body in the church."

It is true that we are not talking about the great universal church now but the local church, the one in your own community, of whose many imperfections and shortcomings you may be well aware. But we must remember that perfection does not exist among human beings, and the institutions they create to the greater glory of God are filled with these selfsame flaws. Jesus is the only perfect Man who ever lived. The rest of us are at best but repentant sinners, try as we may to follow His magnificent example; and the church is but turning a blind eye toward itself when it claims infallibility or perfection for itself or any of its members.

When Jesus founded the church, He intended His fol-

[8] *Hebrews 10:25.*

lowers to join it and remain faithful to it. Today, if you
are among the forty-one per cent of the population of this
country who have no formal church affiliation, you may
stand in bewilderment before the number whose membership is open to you. In selecting one you may well
have a natural tendency to return to the church of your
childhood, or you may feel you want to make a choice
based on your more spiritually mature judgment. A
church affiliation is not something to be entered into
lightly, for if the church is to be of the greatest service to
you, and even more important, if it is to give you the
greatest possible opportunity to be of service to others,
you must prayerfully select the one where you feel you
can be the most service to God.

Whenever anyone points a critical finger and demands
to know why there have to be so many different churches
all serving the same God, I am always tempted to point
out how many different styles of hats have to be designed
for both American men and women. We all belong to the
same human race, but we all have enough physical dif-
ferences to make it impossible for us to wear the same
style of hat with equal satisfaction.

Some people find it easier to draw closer to God in
magnificent buildings and with some form of ritual.
Others find they can seek God only in stark simplicity.
Some people find themselves in sympathy with one kind
of service, others feel more at home in a different atmosphere. The important thing is not *how* we do it, but the
sincerity and depth of purpose *with which* we do it, and
we should each find and join the church in which as individuals we can best accomplish this.

Certainly you would not take up your lifetime abode
in a house without first finding out something about it.
Yet all too many Christians join a church without quite
knowing why, and then, finding it does not meet their
needs, drift on and on, trying them all for a little while,
but coming to secure anchor in none. Such drifting serves
neither the Lord nor themselves.

Churches have different backgrounds, different traditions, different customs, different emphases; and each

Christian should select his church because he is convinced that within its particular structure he will find the greatest opportunities for spiritual growth, the greatest satisfactions for his human needs, and the greatest chance to be of helpful service to those around him.

Do not make the mistake of attaching yourself to a particular minister rather than to the body of the church itself. The ministry may change—it is healthy and stimulating that it should—but the tenets of the church remain the same, and it is to the church and its Christ that you owe allegiance. A stable church is built up when the members of the congregation recognize that it is their mutual love of Jesus Christ and the sincere desire to follow in His steps that hold them together.

The true Christian does not go to church because it's fashionable, because it gives him standing in the community, because it publicly stamps him as a just and righteous person. The true Christian doesn't even go to church because it eases his soul and brings him peace, although that is certainly one of the rich rewards of church membership.

The true Christian goes to church not only for what he gets out of it, but also for what he can put into it. He goes to add his prayers to those of others, he goes to add his voice to the other voices raised in praise of the Lord, he goes to add his strength in beseeching the Lord's blessing, he goes to add his weight of testimony to the possibility of salvation through the Lord Jesus Christ. He goes to join with others in the worship of God, in the contemplation of His boundless mercy and love.

The purpose of this Christian society called the "church" is, First: *to glorify God by our worship.* We do not go to church just to hear a sermon. We go to church to worship God. We are to worship Him in spirit and in truth. The symbols, the songs, the messages of worship are there to help us glorify God in the act of worship. The chief end of man is to glorify God. We glorify Him more by our worship than by any other possible means. Christian activity, soul winning, Bible reading, and a thousand and one good activities of the church cannot take the place of worship. Worship is absolutely necessary if we are to live a happy Christian life. God wants our worship and praise more than any other thing.

Second: *the church is for fellowship.* Probably the greatest foretaste of heaven here on earth is the fellowship that Christians have one with another. If you are a true Christian, you will look forward with keen anticipation to your next contact with other Christians. In the early days most of the social life of the community centered around the church. That does not mean that church buildings are to be turned into playhouses, poolrooms, or bowling alleys. Every activity of the church should be carried on under the direction of Christ to glorify God, but we as Christians need each other. We need each other's prayers and help. We have a responsibility toward each other.

Paul likens the church to the body. The hand has its obligation toward the lips, the eye must work in unison with the ear, the feet must act in harmony with the hand, every member of the body must bear its own burden; but it also must co-operate in bearing the burdens of every other member of the body.

Christianity is a religion of fellowship. Following Christ means love, righteousness, service, and these can be achieved and expressed through social relations. That social relationship is to be found in the church. It is through fellowship that we strengthen each other. Jesus said, "Where two or three are gathered together in My name, there am I in the midst." [4] Jesus was teaching our need of praying and worshiping together as a social group.

Third: *the church is for the strengthening of faith.* Through joint prayers, testimonies, and the preaching and the teaching of the various organizations of the church, your faith will be strengthened. The church will build you up in the most holy faith by re-emphasizing the points that we have already covered in "The Rules for the Christian Life."

[4] *Matthew 18:20.*

Fourth: *the church is a medium of service*. We are saved to serve. There are a thousand and one tasks to be done for Christ. This work can best be accomplished through the fellowship of a local church. A virile Christianity has never existed apart from the church. The church is the organization of Christ upon earth. The church, with all of its imperfections, failures, and divisions is still the church. No other organization will ever take its place.

Fifth: *the church should be the means of channeling your funds for Christian work*. The Bible teaches tithing. A tithe is one tenth of your net income. That one tenth of your income belongs to the Lord. In addition to your tithe, you should give as the Lord has prospered you. Giving is a Christian grace that should be woven into the fabric of our daily lives until it becomes a part no longer distinguishable from the rest. Generosity should motivate us in all things.

Christ said, "It is more blessed to give than to receive." [5] He knew how giving warms the heart and satisfies the soul. He coveted for you that particular blessing. Selfishness is caused by fear—and a Christian should stand forth unafraid. Jesus stood always with hands that were open—not with hands that were clenched tight with selfishness and greed.

Giving cannot be measured in dollars and cents, it cannot be measured in boxes of old clothes. Sometimes the greatest gift is the gift of friendship and neighborliness. A kind word, a friendly greeting, an evening spent with someone who is lonely can reap rich harvest for the kingdom of God. It is impossible for you to become a soul winner unless you are prepared to give something of yourself. Not only your money, but your time, your talents—everything is to be given to the service of Christ.

The giving of your offering which is above the tithe should not be limited by set rules or organized methods. It should be governed by the need that is brought to your attention. It might be a neighbor, the newsboy who

[5] *Acts 20:35.*

brings the daily paper, or someone in far-off Africa or South America. Our giving is the expression of our love for God. We give back to Him in return for the great love that He has bestowed on us, and in that way we spread His love abroad.

There is an art to giving. It is possible to enrich a life with a cup of cold water, or to impoverish a life by giving money without love. Here again the test lies with the giver, for a gift that is given to cause another to be indebted to us is given with far more malice than love. There is no blessing in the gift that is given to show power or domination over another. There is no blessing in a gift that is given grudgingly, or for the calculated effect it will have upon those who witness or are aware of the giving.

We must give willingly, out of a generous desire to bring help and comfort—not with the thought of how the gift may work to our own benefit. We must give kindly and wisely lest our gift bring a hurt instead of a benediction. There is a true and lasting joy in giving, a joy of which the selfish and the miserly have no conception, a joy that is denied to the mean and greedy of heart. This is the real joy of sacrifice, a feeling in no way connected with what some like to consider noble self-pity.

Whether our gift be to the Community Chest, the Salvation Army, or a pint of blood to the Red Cross, it should all be given in the name of Jesus Christ. The people to whom it is given should know that you are giving it in the name of Christ. We have too many gifts that are given on a materialistic and secularistic basis today. The gift of a Christian should be a special gift. The letter accompanying the financial gift to the social or charitable organization should say, "I am giving this in the name of Jesus Christ, my blessed Lord." This provides a testimony to those who are handling the funds. Therefore you are killing two birds with one stone—you are providing the financial gift and at the same time spreading the gospel of good news.

Be careful that you do not become guilty of the sin of robbing God. The Bible says, "Bring ye all the tithes into the storehouse, that there may be meat in Mine house, and prove Me now herewith, saith the Lord of hosts, if I will not open you the windows of heaven, and pour you out a blessing, that there shall not be room enough to receive it." [6]

Dr. Louis Evans has said, "The gospel is free, but it costs money to provide the pails in which to carry the water of salvation."

The act of giving is just as much an act of worship as praying or singing. The United States Government now allows us to give twenty per cent of our income free of tax. It is deductible from our income tax, and yet it is estimated that less than ten per cent of the American people take advantage of this. Corporations are allowed to give five per cent and yet only about fifteen per cent of them are taking advantage of this provision of the government. We should be ashamed of ourselves.

The entire world could be evangelized overnight if Christian people would give as the Lord has prospered them. Be a generous giver, and God has promised that He will return it to you a hundred-fold. Jesus promises one hundred per cent return on your investment. Do you know any bank or financial institution that will give you one hundred per cent increase on the money invested? God says prove me now, see what I'll do. Give until it hurts and see what God will give you in return.

Sixth: *the church is for the spreading of the gospel.* The church is commanded to "Go ye into all the world, and preach the gospel," and to baptize those who believe. The basic and primary mission of the church is to proclaim Christ to the lost. The world today is sending forth its S.O.S., asking the church to come to its help. The world is being overwhelmed by social, moral, and economic problems. Its people are going down, swept under the waves of crime and shame. The world needs Christ. The mission of the church is to throw the life line to the perishing sinners everywhere.

Jesus said, "Ye shall receive power, after that the Holy

[6] *Malachi 3:10.*

Ghost is come upon you: and ye shall be witnesses." [7]
With the power of the Holy Spirit we can join hands
with other Christians to win people to Christ. Sixty-five
per cent of the world has yet to hear the gospel of Jesus
Christ. In this generation we have failed miserably to
spread the gospel to a needy world. There are still over a
thousand languages and dialects into which the Bible has
not been translated.

The early church had no Bibles, no seminaries, no
printing presses, no literature, no educational institutions,
no radio, no television, no automobiles, no airplanes; and
yet within one generation the gospel had been spread to
most of the known world. The secret of the spread of this
gospel was the power of the Holy Spirit.

Today in the face of vastly improved methods of communication the power of the Holy Spirit is being neglected. We are trying to do things in our own strength,
and as a result we are failing. Millions of Americans are
pagan, idolatrous. They are worshiping at the shrines of
secularism, materialism, and sinful pleasure; and all the
time the church hears the command of Christ to "Go."
The hour is getting late! The world is rushing madly on
its way toward destruction! The only hope for a war-mad
world is the gospel of Jesus Christ.

The only feet that Christ has are your feet. The only
hands that He has are your hands. The only tongue that
He has is your tongue. Use every talent, facility, and
method possible to win men to Christ. This is the great
mission of the church. Our methods may vary. We may
use visitation evangelism, education evangelism, preaching missions, industrial evangelism, cell evangelism, radio-
television evangelism, movie evangelism, or so-called
mass evangelism. Whatever it may be, let us use it to win
other people to Christ.

But to get a person committed to make a decision for
Christ is not enough. We must get him into the fellowship of the church so that he may grow in grace and
knowledge of the Lord Jesus Christ. This is evangelism

[7] *Acts* 1:8.

at its best—an evangelism that demands total commitment with a follow-up program that gets the individual
into the various activities of the church.

Finally: *it is through the church that our humanitarianism finds its widest expression.* We are in truth our brothers' keepers, and one has only to visit some of the non-
Christian countries to be impressed with the fact that
it is this teaching above all others, perhaps, that sets the
followers of Christ apart from those who know Him not.

The story of the Good Samaritan was told by Jesus to
etch His humanitarian commands forever in our minds,
and no Christian worthy of the name can ignore the
needs of others simply because his own welfare is not
affected. In some eastern countries it is not uncommon to
see human suffering, human justice, and human needs ig-
nored. A child may sit starving on the street in full view
of passing throngs, yet because the child is no one's im-
mediate responsibility, no one will feel called upon to do
anything until the child is dead and the body must be removed. Such indifference to human misery is intolerable
to a Christian.

In ministering to the hungry, to the naked, to the sick,
and to the imprisoned and enslaved, we should remember always that Jesus Himself told us that in turning a
deaf ear to human suffering wherever we find it, in being
indifferent to human wrongs and callous to human injustice, we are in truth turning a deaf ear to Him. "Verily,
I say unto you, Inasmuch as ye did it not to one of the
least of these, ye did it not to me." [8]

We have but to look about us at the many hospitals,
homes for orphans, aged, and helplessly poverty-stricken,
which have been organized by churches, to recognize
how powerfully this teaching has taken hold. We revere
nursing and social service as one of the highest calling;
but in some parts of the world, where the teachings of
Jesus Christ have not yet penetrated, only the lowest of
social outcasts are permitted to minister to the sick.

Church members should feel a sense of outrage at lax

[8] *Matthew 25:45.*

public health measures, even though their own families may not be endangered. United church action can and frequently does become an important instrument in correcting abuses of civil power and in raising community standards. Whether it is a campaign for more honest law enforcement or better garbage disposal, the cause of humanity at large is being served, and constructive service is one of the first duties of the church just as it is for every sincere member of it. The example of the Good Samaritan, who offered a helping hand first, without asking, "What am I going to get out of this?" should be every true Christian's measure of service to his brothers.

As we said at the beginning of this chapter, man is by nature a social animal. He does his best work, accomplishes his mightiest deed, develops his best self-discipline in the company of others. Anyone who has ever undertaken to lose weight by exercise is well aware of how much more faithful he is about doing the exercises when he does them in a group than by himself!

Because we are human, because we are imperfect and wayward children, we need the support of each other to help keep us on the right track. The long road is less lonely when it is shared by companions who are seeking the same destination; the heavy burdens are lighter when they are lifted in the company of others who are carrying equal loads. It is within the church that this fellowship is found. It is within the church that each Christian soul finds a spiritual home and a focal point for all human activities. Jesus knew well how much we human beings need to work and live and find relaxation and recreation within a group. The church is that group to which He bids everyone become a part.

Chapter Sixteen

SOCIAL OBLIGATIONS
OF THE CHRISTIAN

*And as ye would that men should do to you, do ye
also to them likewise.*

LUKE 6:31.

SINCE you have made your decision for Christ and have
begun studying the Bible, you find yourself confronted
with various social obligations and problems. You have
made your peace with God. You are no longer at war and
at enmity with God. Sin has been forgiven. You have
new horizons for your thinking—new perspectives for
your life. The whole world has changed. You now begin
to see others through the eyes of Jesus. Old ideas and
·ideals have changed. Prejudices that you once held are
beginning to slip away. Selfishness that was once char-
acteristic of you in many areas of your life has now gone.

Many people have refused the Christian life because it
has been presented to them in its negative rather than
in its positive aspect. They say that Christian conduct is
against everything that is pleasant and profitable. They
say Christians are like the woman who complained that
everything worth doing in this life is either immoral,
illegal, or fattening!

Contrary to worldly belief, being a true Christian does
not mean the forfeiting of all real pleasure. It is only sinful pleasure that springs from a love of self, rather than
the love of God, or the kind of pleasure that entails a
great outlay of money. The full acceptance of Christ and
the determination to be guided by God's will draws you

almost immediately to the source of the only true pleasure—which is fellowship with Christ. To you who have
not been born again this may seem a far cry from pleasure, but those who have actually experienced daily fellowship with Christ know that it surpasses all worldly
activities.

Even as the Psalmist says, "They shall be abundantly
satisfied with the fatness of Thy house; and Thou shalt
make them drink of the river of Thy pleasures." [1] God
has also said, "No good thing will He withhold from them
that walk uprightly." [2] Paul said that "God hath given us
all things richly to enjoy."

The fact that we have daily fellowship with Christ
should enable us to live realistically. Christ's way of life
does not require that a man renounce any legitimate interests or ambitions. Though the Scriptures may teach
that Christ may return at any time, the Scripture also
exhorts us to carry on business as usual until He comes.

For example, there was nothing wrong about the eating, drinking, marrying, and giving in marriage in Noah's
day except that those activities were perverted to sinful
abuses. Nor was there anything wrong about the buying,
selling, planning, and building in Lot's day except that
they were carried on by sinful methods. What seems to
have been fundamentally wrong in the days of Noah and
Lot was that men made these the *sole* interest of their
lives. They thought of nothing but their personal pleasures, their personal property, and the material profits
they were amassing. They became so absorbed in the
things of this life that they had no time for God. This was
displeasing to God and He visited the offenders with
judgment.

As someone has said, "The Bible was not written to encourage people to take an interest in the affairs of this
life. It *assumes* that they already have more than their
share of interest of that. The Bible aims to encourage man
to see his worldly affairs in the light of the greater importance and value of spiritual things."

[1] *Psalm 36:8.*   [2] *Psalm 84:11.*

The Bible teaches that we are to perform our daily tasks and that we are to take pride in performing them well. We were put here on earth and given certain work to do, and those who claim that they are Christians are taught not only to labor but to labor to the best of their ability.

The Bible speaks approvingly of Bezaleel as a worker in metals, stone, and wood. Jacob and his sons were shepherds. Joseph was a prime minister. Daniel was a statesman. Both Joseph and Jesus were carpenters, and some of the disciples were fishermen. We are told of the Ethiopian eunuch who was treasurer under Candace; of Lydia, the seller of purple; of Paul, Priscilla, and Aquila who were tentmakers; and Luke, the physician.

The Christian ideal certainly does not demand that man renounce all interest in the affairs of this life; but rather that he seek God's guidance in performing his daily work to the best of his ability, and that he keep both his work and his ambitions in subordination to the Lord at all times. Thus we find that Christ offers positive help in our daily living here on earth. He helps in our work and in our pleasure.

He also helps in facing the social problems that confront us and it is here that we may become confused. For it is in our daily tasks and in the way we face the social problems around us that the world will see Christ in us.

As Dr. L. Nelson Bell says in the *Southern Presbyterian Journal*, "If you are in church on Sunday the people who see you there may *presume* that you are a Christian. But what about the people with whom you come in contact during the week on the street, in your office, in your store, and the multiple places where you make these inevitable daily contacts? Orthodox Christian profession has its place. Attendance at, and active participation in, the program and activities of the church are an inescapable part of Christian living. But as we all know, the business of making a living, the responsibilities of a home, the daily routine all combine to test the reality of our Christian experience and faith. In these daily contacts what do others see? Can our week-day associates tell that we are Christians? Do casual acquaintances see anything in us to suggest that we are different from those who do not know Christ? Certainly one of the real tests of Christian character is to be found in the lives we live from day to day.

"The reality of our Christian profession is shown in many ways: the things we say, as well as the things we do not say; the things we do, as well as the things we do not do. For while Christianity is not primarily a matter of externals, nevertheless it does find expression in conversation, habits, recreation, emphasis, and ambitions to be noted in our daily life. Does our conversation honor Christ? Are our habits those of which He approves? Are our sources of recreation those in which His presence can be a part? Do we bow our heads in a word of thanks when eating in a public place? Can people tell from the emphasis we attach to material things whether we have set our affection on things above, or whether we are primarily attached to this world? Do people see in us an ambition for place and position out of accord with that of a Christian? We should ask ourselves these and many other questions, for in such things men judge whether we are Christians or not."

What is our attitude toward the race question? What is our attitude toward sex? What is our attitude toward the labor-management problems? What is our attitude toward tolerance? All of these are very real and practical questions that must be answered, interpreted, and lived before our fellow men.

The guiding principle of our relation to the world about us should be, "And as ye would that men should do to you, do ye also to them likewise." [3]

Many people have criticized the so-called "social gospel," but Jesus taught that we are to take regeneration in one hand and a cup of cold water in the other. Christians, above all others, should be concerned with social problems and social injustices. Down through the centuries the church has contributed more than any other

[3] *Luke 6:31.*

single agency in lifting social standards to new heights. Child labor has been outlawed. Slavery has been abolished. The status of woman has been lifted to heights unparalleled in history, and many other reforms have taken place as a result of the influence of the teachings of Jesus Christ. The Christian is to take his place in society with moral courage to stand up for that which is right, just, and honorable.

First: *the Christian should be a good citizen.* The Bible teaches that the Christian should be law-abiding. The Bible also teaches loyalty to country. A loyalty and love of country does not mean that we cannot criticize certain unjust laws that may discriminate against special groups. The Bible says that God is no respecter of persons. All should have equal opportunities. The government of God is to be our model.

The Bible also teaches that we are to co-operate with the government. Jesus was asked, "Is it lawful to give tribute?" Jesus set the example forever by paying taxes. It takes money to run a government and to maintain law and order. The tax dodger is a civic parasite and an actual thief. No true Christian will be a tax dodger. Jesus said, we are to "render to Caesar the things that are Caesar's." [4] We ought to be more than taxpayers. To be simply law-abiding is not enough. We ought to seek and work for the good of our country. Sometimes we may be called upon to die for it. We are to do it gladly—as unto God. We are to be conscientious in our work as good citizens.

We should be philanthropic and give to charitable organizations that are doing good for the betterment of mankind. We should enter into various activities such as the Community Chest, the Red Cross, the Salvation Army, and other good, constructive, and helping-hand organizations. Christians should be interested in orphanages, hospitals, asylums, prisons, and all social institutions. Jesus said, "Love thy neighbor as thyself." [5] Think of a country without any philanthropic enterprises what-

[4] *Mark 12:17.*   [5] *Matthew 22:39.*

ever! No one would want to live in it. We want to live
where neighborly love prevails. We are to take our place
in the community. Those in positions of responsibility
are entitled to respect, support, and co-operation. "Let
every soul be subject unto the higher powers. For there
is no power but of God: the powers that be are ordained
of God." [6]

Second: *Christians should be "given to hospitality."* [7]
The Bible teaches that our homes should be open to all
and that those who come in and out of our homes should
sense the presence of Christ. That which God has given
to us should be shared with others. In doing so God will
bless and prosper our homes.

Third: *we should have the Christian attitude toward
sex.* Nowhere does the Bible teach that sex in itself is a
sin, although many interpreters of the Bible would try to
make it appear so. The Bible teaches that the *wrong use*
of sex is sinful. For sex, the act by which all life on this
earth is created, should be the most wonderful, the most
meaningful, the most satisfying of human experiences.

Man, with his vile, self-destructive nature, however,
has taken what was intended to be the most glorious and
complete act of love between two people, and made of it
something low and cheap and filthy. Sex, stripped of
mutual love, respect, and the sincere desire to give joy
and fulfillment to the other person, becomes simply an
animal act, about which the Bible warns us in no un-
certain terms!

It is significant that the Bible is one of the world's most
outspoken books on the subject of sex. It adopts no
"hush-hush" attitude, it does not try to gloss over sex in
either its right or wrong aspects. The sly, secret, embar-
rassed, "let's-pretend-it-doesn't-exist" attitude about sex is
purely man-made.

In trying to overcome the mysterious, "let's-not-talk-
about-it" approach to sex, our present civilization has put
far too much emphasis on the mechanics of it, and far
too little insistence on the spiritual atmosphere in which

[6] *Romans 13:1.*   [7] *1 Timothy 3:2.*

this overwhelming expression of human love must have its origin.

Our divorce courts bear tragic testimony to the inability of men and women to achieve this lasting and ever more beautiful relationship without a firm foundation of spiritual values.

Sex is a part of life that we cannot abolish, even if we would, for without it all life would cease. Used rightly it can bring heaven into the home. Used wrongly it can make it a hell. Use it wisely and it will become a wonderful servant. Use it wrongly and it will be a terrible taskmaster.

Christians feel a sense of outrage, a sense of violation, when they see sex emblazoned in newspaper headlines, exploited in advertisements, and used as a cheap lure outside theaters. They blush for their fellow men that they can be so stupid, so gross, so indecent as to defile and distort the act by which all God-given life is bestowed.

Fourth: it follows naturally that *those who take a Christian view of sex will take a Christian view of marriage*. Before you enter into a marriage, consider the real spiritual implications that make an earthly marriage binding in heaven. Little by little as we grow toward maturity, we learn to love, first our parents and our friends and later the one person who is to share our life. We have already seen how difficult this process is, for it is hate and not love that comes naturally to the unregenerate sinner.

Many have the terrible misfortune of selecting their mates while they are still in the toils of the world, the flesh, and the Devil, and while the man or woman they select is also still in a state of complete sin. Is it any wonder then that so many marriages contracted by two spiritually ignorant souls, incapable of real and lasting love, end up in the divorce courts, making orphans of some seven hundred and fifty thousand children each year?

Marriage is a holy bond because it permits two people to help each other work out their spiritual destinies. God declared marriage to be good because He knew that man needed a helpmate and woman needed a protector. He demands that husbands and wives never lose sight of the

original purpose of marriage. It is woman's role to love
and help and reassure her husband in every way she can,
and it is man's role to love and protect and provide for
his wife and the children she bears, so that the home may
be filled with God's peace and harmony.

Marriages that are entered into with a clear understanding of God's purpose and God's laws have no need
for divorce courts. Marriages that fall short of this ideal
(and it is appalling how many of them do) should first
seek to learn what God expects of the husband and the
wife, and then pray for God's help and guidance in following out His commands.

Fifth: *we are to take the Christian attitude in labor-
management relationships.* The Bible says, "Whatever you
do, put your whole heart and soul into it, as into work
done for God, and not merely for men—knowing that
your real reward, a heavenly one, will come from God,
since you are actually employed by Christ, and not just
by your earthly master. But the slacker and the thief will
be judged by God himself, Who naturally has no distinc-
tion to make between master and man. Remember, then,
you employers, that your responsibility is to be fair and
just towards those whom you employ, never forgetting
that you yourselves have a Heavenly Employer." [8]

If Christ could prevail in all labor-management relations we would not have any strikes. There would not be
these long drawn-out arguments in which both sides are
unwilling to concede the rights of the other. Management
would treat employees with generosity, and employees
would be eager to put in a full day's work for their hire
—for they would not only be working for their wages,
they would be working for God.

The Bible teaches that there is dignity in all types of
honest labor, and the Christian should be the most faithful, the most willing and efficient worker of all. He should
stand out in a factory or shop as one who wants justice,
but one who would not stoop to take unfair advantage.

By the same token, the Christian employer should treat

[8] *Colossians 3:22-25, Phillips translation.*

his employees with a respect and generosity that will become an example for other employers. A man of real Christian concepts cannot help being concerned about safety precautions, good working conditions, and the well-being of those in his employ. He will not only see his workers as "man power," but also as human beings.

Both management and labor should remember that the improved conditions and better understanding they now enjoy had their beginnings as the result of a great spiritual revival. The heritage of labor unions comes from the church and the mighty Wesleyan revivals of the eighteenth century. Social liberty for the working classes began when a Christian leader, Lord Shaftesbury, in the face of bitter family opposition, led a lifelong crusade for better working conditions, shorter hours, more pay, and fair treatment for the working man.

Had it not been for the spiritual revival of the eighteenth century, the gains that labor has made might not have been achieved, or might have been delayed until much later in our history. When some labor leaders talk of outlawing religion, disregarding God, the Bible, and the church, they should remember how much of what they have today is due to the power of the gospel of Christ.

Some labor leaders have grown haughty, proud, rich, self-satisfied, and power-seeking. Many industrialists have done the same. All of them should humble themselves before God, seek to recognize the needs of each other, their extreme dependence on each other, and above all, try to apply the Golden Rule in its most practical and realistic sense.

Sixth: *the Christian looks through the eyes of Christ at the race question* and admits that the church has failed in solving this great human problem. We have let the sports world, the entertainment field, politics, the armed forces, education and industry outstrip us. The church should have been the pace-setter. The church should voluntarily be doing what the federal courts are doing by pressure and compulsion. But in the final analysis the only real solution will be found at the foot of the cross where we come together in brotherly love. The closer the people of all races get to Christ and His cross, the closer they will get to one another.

The Bible says, in Christ there is neither Jew nor Gentile, there is neither male nor female, neither Greek nor barbarian, neither rich nor poor. The Bible indicates that we are all one in Christ. The ground is level at the foot of the cross. When Christ opens our spiritual eyes we behold not color, nor class, nor condition, but simply human beings with the same longings, fears, needs, and aspirations as our own. We begin to see people through the Master's eyes.

Seventh: *the Christian attitude should prevail in the matter of economics.* Jesus said a man's life does not consist in the abundance of the things which he possesses. Money is a good slave but a bad master. Property belongs in the purse or the bank but not in the heart. Wealth has its place and its power, but it is not entitled to occupy the throne or sway the scepter. Covetousness puts money above manhood. It shackles its devotee and makes him its victim. It hardens the heart and deadens the noble impulses and destroys the vital qualities of life.

Beware of covetousness in every phase and form! All of us should keep ourselves from it through vigilance, prayer, self-control, and discipline. Life is not a matter of dollars and cents, houses and lands, earning capacity and financial achievement. Greed must not be allowed to make man the slave of wealth.

When Jesus was asked to settle an inheritance dispute between two brothers, He declined with a word of warning and with one of the magnificent parables with which He so frequently pointed out the earthly applications of heavenly messages. He told the story of the wealthy landowner, who in the midst of prosperity, envisioned even greater wealth and made long-range plans which would fill his life with all the physical comforts and personal glory that he held most dear. Apparently he was talented, economical, industrious, prudent, honest, and moral in all his dealings—but he was the victim of ambition and self-interest, as are so many others.

He measured his success in broad fields and full barns, and fed his soul on human vanities. His life was wrapped up in his riches and centered in himself, and he made his plans without thought of God or the uncertainty of life.

But God spoke the final word, and the plans that extended for years ahead were cut short by sudden death. The property he had amassed so painstakingly slipped through his cold fingers to be divided, scattered, and squandered by others, while he was left to stand before God with nothing to show for the life he had led on earth.

The Christian, above all others, should realize that we come into life with empty hands—and it is with empty hands that we leave it. Actually we can possess nothing—no property and no person—along the way. It is God who owns everything, and we are but stewards of His property during the brief time we are on earth. Everything that we see about us that we count as our possessions only comprises a loan from God, and it is when we lose sight of this all-pervading truth that we become greedy and covetous.

When we clutch an object or a person and say, "This thing is mine," when we look with envious eyes at what another person has and plan to "get it by fair means or foul," we are forgetting that no matter what we get, we can't take it with us when we go to make our final accounting before the seat of judgment.

This does not mean that earthly riches in themselves are a sin—the Bible does not say that. The Bible makes it clear that God expects us to do the best we can with the talents, the abilities, the situations with which life endows us. But as with sex, there is a right way and a wrong way to acquire money and a right way and a wrong way to achieve power. Too many Christians have misunderstood this and taken a most sinful and damaging spiritual pride in being poverty-stricken, in standing by helplessly and saying, "God's will be done," as their children suffered and went untended.

Jesus told one of His most revealing parables to illus-

trate this very point when He recited the story of the rich
man who gave each of his servants a certain amount of
money to invest while he was away in a far land. When
he returned he found that some servants had made wise
investments and his money was multiplied, and he
praised them for their sound judgment and prudence; but
the frightened, unimaginative servant who could think of
nothing to do with the money but to hide it from thieves,
he condemned.

Earn your money, as much as you can, according to
God's laws, and spend it to carry out His commands.
Give one tenth of it to the Lord, tithe faithfully, for the
Bible says that this is right and just. Whenever you have
any doubts about material values, get out your Bible and
read what Jesus taught about money, read what He had
to say about the earning of money and the use and dis-
tribution of wealth. Just ask yourself, "What would Jesus
have done in this situation?" and be guided by that and
that alone.

Eighth: *a Christian will be concerned about suffering
humanity around him.* The great slum areas of your own
country will become a burden to you. The poverty and
suffering of thousands of people in your own neighborhood will become a concern to you. You will join with
organizations and associations to help alleviate the suffering of humanity around you. Many people spend so
much time in lofty enterprises that they make no contribution to suffering immediately at hand.

The Bible says, the common people heard Jesus gladly.
Wherever He went, He healed the sick. He comforted the
sorrowful, He gave practical encouragement. The Christian will be interested in helping build and develop hospitals, orphanages, old people's homes, and other charitable institutions that are trying to help the less fortunate.
The Christian will be interested in doing his part to help
share the great wealth of this country with the needy in
other parts of the world. He will be a supporter of any
national or international social agency helping the unfortunate of the world.

Nowhere in the Bible does it teach that we are to withdraw ourselves from society. Rather, it teaches quite the contrary. We are to join with others who are working to good purpose to help lift the unfortunate. God needs social workers, doctors, hospital attendants, nurses, charity workers, and many other types of people who can help alleviate human suffering.

The motto of the Rotary Club is "Service above self." The motto of the Kiwanis Club is "We build." The motto of the Lions Club is "Liberty, intelligence, our nation's safety." The motto of the Modern Woodmen is "Love thy neighbor." All of these ideas originated in Christianity. Lots of the pagan religions never had a service club. All these organizations are really by-products of Christianity even when some of their members are not Christians. The perfume of Christ is in the fragrance of any and all social service. The ancient world never had a hospital.

Madame Chiang Kai-shek said, "Confucianism worships ancestors but never built an old folks' home." Certainly every Christian should live up to all these mottos. If we did this world would be a better world in which to live. Certainly the motto of Jesus Christ was "love and service"—love for Christ, service for Christ; love for our fellow man, service to our fellow man. Jesus said, "If ye love Me, keep My commandments." [9] In other words, "If you love Me, obey Me! Serve Me!" Christ has a right to test our love for Him by what we are doing for Him. You cannot love without serving.

Ninth: *the Christian has a special obligation to fellow Christians.* Fellow Christians are in a special class. We are *to have supernatural love* for them. "We know that we have passed from death unto life, because we love the brethren. He that loveth not his brother abideth in death." [10]

We are to love our enemies. We are even to love those who persecute us and say "all manner of evil against us, falsely."

But the greatest of our human love is for those other

[9] *John 14:15.*　　　　　　[10] *1 John 3:14.*

Christians. Jesus said, "This is my commandment, that ye love one another, as I have loved you." [11]

We are told *to serve* one another, "Brethren, through love be servants of one another."

> Lord, help me to live from day to day
> In such a self-forgetful way
> That even when I kneel to pray
> My prayers shall be for others.
>
> Help me in all the work I do
> Ever to be sincere and true,
> And know that all I do for Thee
> Must needs be done for others.
>
> Others, Lord; yes, others.
> Let this my motto be.
> Let me live for others
> That I may live like Thee.

The Bible says that our obligation to each other as Christians is such that we should *be examples* to each other. Paul said, "Be thou an example of the believers, in word, in conversation, in charity, in spirit, in faith, in purity." [12] This is not a suggestion—but a command! It is not a recommendation, but an obligation. We are to be model Christians.

The Bible also says we are *to forgive* one another. "And be ye kind one to another, tenderhearted, forgiving one another, even as God for Christ's sake hath forgiven you." [13] Jesus said that if you will not forgive, neither will your Father which is in heaven forgive your sins. He also said "When ye stand praying, forgive, if you have ought against any; that your Father also may forgive you." [14]

We are told as Christians *not to judge* one another, but

[11] *John 15:12.*   [12] *1 Timothy 4:12.*
[13] *Ephesians 4:32.*   [14] *Mark 11:25.*

rather decide never to put a stumbling block or hindrance in the way of a brother.

The Bible says that we are *to be subject* one to another; we are to clothe ourselves with humility toward each other. We are to be "in honor, preferring one another." We are to put others first, and ourselves last.

As Christians we are *to bear one another's burdens.* There are burdens which every man must bear for himself for no one can do it for him, and if he neglects them they will not be borne. There is the burden of being honest—of obeying God's Word—of training your children for God—of making your wife happy. In all such cases one must bear his own burdens. But there are other burdens that our friends can help us bear, such as sorrow, misfortune, trials, loneliness, family cares, spiritual difficulties, and official responsibilities. But we are not to worry about our burdens. We are to roll them on to God's shoulders, looking to Him for power to sustain and strengthen us. However, it is our duty to help our fellow man bear his own burden.

The Bible says as Christians also we are *to be liberal* with each other. God says it is our duty as Christians to take care of widows and orphans, and to help the poor within the Christian society. The Bible says: contribute to the needs of the saints . . . practice hospitality . . . lodge strangers . . . wash the saints' feet . . . relieve the afflicted . . . be not forgetful to entertain strangers. And Jesus said, "Inasmuch as ye have done it unto one of the least of these my brethren, ye have done it unto me. . . . It is more blessed to give than to receive." "God loveth a cheerful giver." All of these are our social obligations one to another as Christians.

Lastly, Christians ought *to be gracious,* and this is one of the most difficult of Christian virtues. The very power of our conviction inclines us toward feeling that we are right and that all other people are wrong. This is well and good when our convictions are based upon the "Thou shalts" and the "Thou shalt nots" of Scripture rather than our own ideas. The many different and frequently warring factions within the church emphasize the terrible human tendency to gather into select little groups, built upon profound convictions on trivial matters, each insisting that they and they alone have the right answer.

As the late Dr. Harry Ironside once said: "Beware lest we mistake our prejudices for our convictions."

To be sure we must deplore wickedness, evil and wrongdoing, but our commendable intolerance of sin too often develops into a deplorable intolerance of sinners.

I was amused and shocked to hear a man of considerable religious background declare on television not long ago that "you didn't catch Jesus associating with questionable people or those whose basic ideas and attitudes were at variance with what Jesus knew to be honorable and right!"

Such a man should have known that Jesus wasn't afraid to associate with anyone! One of the things which the scribes and Pharisees criticized most bitterly was His willingness to help and talk and exchange ideas with anyone, be they publicans, thieves, learned professors or prostitutes, rich or poor! Even His own followers decried some of the people with whom He was seen in public, but this did not lessen the compassion that Jesus felt for all the members of poor, blinded, struggling humanity.

Jesus had the most open and all-encompassing mind that this world has ever seen. His own inner conviction was so strong, so firm, so unswerving that He could afford to mingle with any group secure in the knowledge that He would not be contaminated. It is fear that makes us unwilling to listen to another's point of view, fear that our own ideas may not be unassailable. Jesus had no such fear, no such pettiness of viewpoint, no need to fence himself off for His own protection. He knew the difference between graciousness and compromise and we would do well to learn of Him. He set for us the most magnificent and glowing example of truth combined with mercy of all time, and in departing said: "Go ye and do likewise."

These are just a few of the scores of things that could be mentioned that are the social obligations of the Christian. He cannot withdraw himself as a hermit and live a solitary life. He is a member of society. Therefore, the teachings of Jesus are full of our attitudes toward our fellow men.

Study the Bible, read it—and then live by it. Only then can you demonstrate to a confused world the transforming power of the indwelling Christ.

Chapter Seventeen

THE FUTURE OF THE CHRISTIAN

*I go to prepare a place for you. And if I go and pre-
pare a place for you, I will come again, and receive
you unto myself; that where I am, there ye may be
also.*

JOHN 14:2-3.

THE world unites in testifying that we are in an hour
of dire crisis. Many are predicting impending calamities.
Some say that the race is heading toward destruction.
Many believe we are on the verge of the eclipse of civilization itself.

Many of the best-selling books deal with dire predictions of the future. Editorials in newspapers and maga-
zines are talking about Armageddon, the end of time and
the destruction of civilization. A president in his inaugu-
ral says, "Science has bequeathed to us the ability to
destroy ourselves." Mr. William Vogt in his book, *Road
to Survival,* says, "The handwriting on the wall of five
continents now tells us that the day of judgment is at
hand." Dr. Richard K. Ullmann has written: "We live in
an age of decision, of choice between right and wrong,
between good and evil, between life and death, such as
has never occurred before. If we choose wrongly, we may
be the last generation of mankind."

Professor Sorokin has said: "We live amidst one of the
greatest crises in human history. Not only war, famine,
pestilence, and revolution, but a legion of other calamities
are also rampant over the whole world. All values are
unsettled. All norms are broken. Humanity has become a
distorted image of its own noble self. The crisis is omni-

present and involves almost the whole of culture and society from top to bottom. It is manifest in the fine arts and science, in philosophy and religion, in ethics and law. It permeates the forms of social, economic and political organizations and the entire way of living and thinking. There is every reason to expect that the disastrous effects of such calamities will fall upon us in a much more intensive and extensive scale during this catastrophic age of ours."

As we move through the vast literature created by the atomic and hydrogen bombs—the books and articles that, on one hand, describe the experiments in Nevada and Bikini; and, on the other hand, those that attempt to portray something of the inescapable crisis that is now facing the human race—we are amazed to find that science is now using Biblical terminology. As Dr. Wilbur Smith says, "Plato, Seneca, Aristotle and practically none of the great philosophers ever attempted to delve into the future." The Bible is the only Book in the world that has an eschatology. From Genesis to Revelation the Bible is full of the events that await the climax of history. For the past few years church leaders have been afraid of fanaticism in the discussion of future events, but the church is taking a new look at these reams of Holy Scripture that talk about the future-events' course of human history.

The World Council of Churches, for its meeting at Evanston in 1954, chose as its theme: "Christ, The Hope of the World." The World Council appointed committees to study the teachings of the Bible in order that the church might present an adequate picture of God's revelation concerning the future.

At a moment like this men and women who are untaught in the Bible are prone, as in every preceding critical hour, to become the dupes of false prophets, spiritualism, palm readers, tea leaf readers, and other forms of superstitions. Thousands of dollars are being spent daily by frightened people trying to find some inkling as to what the future holds. All they have to do is go to the nearest book shop and purchase an inexpensive Bible and find within its pages the secrets of the future.

There is not one sentence in Mary Baker Eddy's *Science and Health* that throws any light on the future. You can read the *Koran* from cover to cover and not find a word concerning the future of mankind. It is the Bible, and the Bible alone, that casts a penetrating light into the darkness and mystery of the future.

The veil of mystery is lifted, the future is revealed—the Bible predicts that there is coming an end to this world system as we know it. The Bible declares that the climax of history will be the coming again of Jesus Christ. The Bible gives hints that the greatest coronation of all time will take place when Christ is crowned King of Kings and Lord of Lords.

I am aware of the fact that this is a controversial and often misunderstood subject. We have had a great many fanatics in past years who have gone about the country setting dates, and as a result this glorious truth has been obscured.

The magazine *Religion in Life* carried an article entitled "The Christian Hope—Its Meaning For Today." The subject of the future was discussed by three intellectual leaders. One is Dr. Arnold J. Toynbee, the famous British historian; another is Dr. Amos N. Wilder, well-known theologian at the University of Chicago; and the other is Dr. C. S. Lewis, famed English scholar and professor at Oxford University.

Toynbee sees a world divided into two camps as a result of technological changes which have made all men neighbors without giving them tolerance, love, and understanding of one another. The Christian hope, according to Toynbee, is to fight the leviathan of man-worship, materialism, and collectivism.

Dr. Wilder, on the other hand, doubts if man can find the Christian hope within history itself. Redemption, he believes, must come from spiritual resources outside the human race. Man must realize that God's purposes will eventually be worked out in the world even if it requires the refining fires of war and tragedy. Man will someday build a kingdom of God on earth largely through his own strength and wisdom.

It is not until we come to the statement by Dr. Lewis that we feel that we are on a Biblical basis for thinking. Lewis accepts God's Word as the truth. He frankly declares, "It seems to me impossible to retain in any recognizable form our belief in the divinity of Christ and the truth of the Christian revelation while abandoning or deducting the promised and threatened return of Jesus Christ."

Dr. Lewis points out three reasons why people scoff at the idea of the return of Jesus Christ to this earth: *first*, many professed Christians say it is a false teaching since the second coming of Jesus Christ did not take place as the early church predicted. It is true that the early Christians looked for the Lord's return in their time, but many prophecies of the Bible were to be fulfilled before the second coming, says Lewis. *Second*, the theory of evolution keeps many people from believing the doctrine of the second coming of Christ. If we believe man is progressing upward of himself, we will never accept the promise of Christ that He will return and bring an end to sin and death. *Third*, he points out the doctrine that Christ is coming cuts across the plans and dreams of millions of people. They want to eat, drink, and be merry without interference in their selfish course of action.

This was exactly the reason why the scoffers of Noah's time refused to believe in a flood, for they did not wish anything to mar their selfish plans for the future. The Bible itself predicted that scoffers would come in the last days with scoffing, following their own passions, and saying, "Where is the promise of His coming? for since the fathers fell asleep, all things continue as they were from the beginning of the creation." [1]

The whole point of God's offer of hope and of God's warning would have been lost if, in departing, He had left behind the exact date of His return. It is because we know not at what hour He will return that we must keep our spiritual houses in readiness at all times.

[1] *2 Peter 3:4.*

The great D. L. Moody used to say, "I never preach a sermon without thinking that possibly the Lord may come before I preach another."

Dr. G. Campbell Morgan, the distinguished British clergyman, said, "I never begin my work in the morning without thinking that perhaps He may interrupt my work and begin His own. I am not looking for death. I am looking for Him."

That's the way a Christian should live his life, in the constant anticipation of the return of Jesus Christ! If we could live every day as though it might be the very last one before the final judgment, what a difference it would make here on earth!

But we don't like to think that way! We don't like to think that our carefully made plans, our long-range schemes may be interrupted by the trumpets of God! We're so engrossed in our own little activities that we can't bear the thought of having anything spoil them! Too many people would rather say, "Oh well, the end of the world hasn't come yet, so why think about it—it's probably a thousand years away!"

It may be! But on the other hand, it may not! I'm not going to predict the end of the world. Too many well-meaning people have done that and been guilty of tragic disservice to the Christian cause. Too many religious cranks and fanatics have held Christian faith up to ridicule by making false predictions.

Students of religious history can recall all too vividly the many times that self-styled prophets have created mass hysteria. Back in 1843, William Miller predicted that the end of the world would occur on the night of March 21. At exactly midnight, he declared, the trumpets would sound, the heavens would roll up like a great scroll, and Jesus would appear for the second time! Those who believed William Miller, instead of the Bible, gathered in a great crowd and waited, and then slipped home in the early morning light, disappointed and ashamed.

They could have been saved this public embarrassment had they but recalled the warning that Jesus uttered over and over, "Watch ye therefore: for *ye know not* when the master of the house cometh, at even, or at midnight, or at the cockcrowing, or in the morning: Lest coming suddenly He find you sleeping. And what I say unto you, I say unto all, Watch." [2]

Both false predictions and human unwillingness to admit that life on this earth may come to a sudden halt, because of supernatural forces quite outside ourselves, have made many people scoff at the idea of the second coming.

There is still another reason which has lulled too much of the "civilized" world into an unwarranted feeling of security. It is the erroneous doctrine of "progress"! According to this teaching, man and all his works are slowly and painfully making their way upward by their own strength and intelligence. Many who believe in this theory also claim to believe in the second coming of Christ, but they say this coming means only the day when man will have purified himself by his own means! When he will have come to recognize the futility of war, the stupidity of greed and selfish behavior, the uselessness of prejudice and intolerance, and clearly understands that he *is* his brother's keeper and must live according to the Golden Rule!

This myth—for the theory of inevitable "progress" is a myth and nothing more—is based on what man *hopes* is happening and not on what is really taking place. When such men point to the fact that modern medicine is now making it possible for us to live longer than our ancestors, they overlook the fact that death is still our ultimate destiny. At best, we have only been able to postpone it for a few brief years.

When they point to our vastly improved transportation and communications systems, they try to ignore the fact that we have used our conquest of the air mainly to carry death and destruction to our fellow men and not to spread the gospel and Christian faith.

When they boast of our far-flung network of schools and colleges, they quickly pass over the fact that much

[2] *Mark* 13:35-37.

of the teaching in these schools and colleges has led students further from, instead of closer to, God.

These men exalt the ingenious minds that have finally solved the mystery of the atom, while we tremble at the thought of what this, the zenith of man's cleverness, may have brought upon us all!

These are among the high points of man's "progress." These are the achievements from which some men take hope, on which some men pin their faith of a better and more peaceful world. They seem to take it for granted that "progress" leads always toward improvement, when in reality it can lead backwards as well as ahead!

What, then, are the arguments on the other side? What sure proof do we have that Jesus will return and that we should live our lives in constant readiness for the glorious day?

The Bible is our proof, of course, and in the Scripture the second coming of Christ is given a most prominent place. Some Bible students have shown that one out of every thirty verses mentions this doctrine, and for every *one* mention of the first coming of Christ there are *eight* references to His second coming! In all, there are three hundred and eighteen references to it. In the Old Testament it is the theme of the prophets, and in the New Testament whole books (1 and 2 Thessalonians) and entire chapters (Matthew 24; Mark 13; Luke 21) are devoted to it.

The whole Bible emphasizes over and over the fact that Christ will come back. For example, in Isaiah (66:15) we are told that "the Lord will come with fire, and with His chariots like a whirlwind, to render His anger with fury, and His rebuke with flames of fire."

In Jeremiah, we are told that at the Lord's coming Jerusalem will be made the throne of His glory and nations shall be gathered in representation. There shall be a mighty disarmament conference in Jerusalem, far greater than any the world has ever seen in Washington or London or Paris!

Ezekiel tells of Jerusalem which is to be restored, a

temple which is to be rebuilt, and a land which is to be reclaimed and filled with prosperity.

Daniel saw Him in visions, coming as the Judge and King of the earth.

Hosea says that in the latter times when the Lord shall return, Israel shall accept Him as Lord and King.

Joel describes the world's armies arrayed in the last day against the host of heaven.

Amos reveals the new throne of David established again in Jerusalem.

Obadiah issues serious warnings in view of the coming again of the Prince of Princes.

Micah announces the cessation of all wars when swords shall be beaten into plowshares and spears into pruning-hooks.

Nahum tells of the mountains quaking beneath His feet and the very earth burning with the presence of Christ.

Habakkuk shows the King measuring the new Kingdom with a measuring rod and all the hills bowing unto Him.

Zephaniah gives us the new song that He will teach unto Israel and describes the overthrow of the false Christ.

Haggai tells of the shaking of all things and only the things of God remaining.

Zechariah gives the picture of His feet standing again on the Mount of Olives. The mountain shall split in twain and the valley of decision shall be formed.

Malachi closes the Old Testament story of the coming Prince by showing Him as a refiner's fire and as a fuller's soap, and as the rising sun filling the whole earth with His glory. The Old Testament is brimming with accounts of the second coming of Christ.

In the New Testament the predictions of His coming are even more vivid and couched in even clearer terms. Matthew likens Christ to a bridegroom coming to receive his bride.

Mark sees Him as a householder going on a long journey and committing certain tasks to his servants until his return.

To Luke, Jesus is a nobleman going into a far country to transact certain businesses and leaving his possessions with his servants in order that they might trade with them until he comes.

John quotes Christ as saying, "I go and prepare a place for you, I will come again, and receive you unto myself."

In Romans we see Him at His coming placing all things beneath His feet.

In 1 Corinthians, Paul tells of the Lord's coming to awaken and raise the dead; 2 Corinthians describes the new house we shall have when this earthly house is dissolved.

Colossians (3:4) says, "When Christ, Who is our life, shall appear, then shall ye also appear with Him in Glory."

In 1 Thessalonians, Paul tells us to wait for God's Son from heaven. 2 Thessalonians gives us the glorious picture of the Lord coming with His saints.

In Timothy, we find these words, that the Lord will reward all those who "love His appearing."

Titus talks about the "blessed hope."

Hebrews tells about His coming the second time apart from sin.

James urges his readers to be patient unto the coming of the Lord.

Peter says that the day of the Lord cometh as a thief in the night.

John gives the great promise to all believers, "Now are we the sons of God, and it doth not yet appear what we shall be: but we know that, when He shall appear, we shall be like Him, for we shall see Him as He is."

Jude says, "Behold the Lord cometh with ten thousands of His saints."

And the whole Book of Revelation is given over to the teaching of the coming of Jesus Christ.

Not only does the Old Testament tell us to expect the second coming of Christ, not only is the New Testament filled with the promise of it, but if we would study the historic documents of our major denominations, we would find that our founders all believed and accepted it.

The most thrilling, glorious truth in all the world is the second coming of Jesus Christ. It is the sure promise of the future, when all about us is pessimism and gloom. When people wail, "What is to become of us, whither are we drifting?" the Bible can give them a sure, straight answer. The Bible says that the consummation of all things shall be the coming again of Jesus Christ, and the rewards that await the elect of God!

As to the exact time and date that this glorious event will occur, I would not defy Providence by hazarding a guess! I know too well that passage in Acts 1:6,7, when the disciples asked, "Lord, wilt thou at this time restore again the kingdom to Israel?" And Jesus answered saying, "It is not for you to know the times or the seasons, which the Father hath put in His own power."

It is not important that we know the exact time of His coming. What is important is that we live our lives in such a way as to be ready for it at any moment! Jesus said that the angels in heaven did not know, that only God Himself is aware of the hour and the moment when the mighty blasts shall be heard, the heavens shall part and Christ and His heavenly host shall appear once more to human eyes!

Jesus did, however, say that there would be certain trends that might indicate that the time of His second appearance was drawing near. He said, "And when these things begin to come to pass, then look up, and lift up your heads: for your redemption draweth nigh. And He spake to them a parable: Behold the fig tree, and all the trees; When they now shoot forth, ye see and know of your own selves that summer is now nigh at hand. So likewise ye, when ye see these things come to pass, know ye that the kingdom of God is nigh at hand." [3]

And what were these trends that Jesus bid us look and watch for? "And there shall be signs in the sun, and in the moon, and in the stars; and upon the earth distress

[3] *Luke 21:28-31.*

of nations, with perplexity: the sea and the waves roaring; Men's hearts failing them for fear, and for looking after those things which are coming on the earth: for the powers of heaven shall be shaken." (Luke 21:25-26.)

Time, as measured by the angels who view all eternity, is far different from the earthly calendar by which we reckon it. To us who clutch desperately to our allotted three score years and ten, to us who see the days in relation to our own particular stay on earth, to us a hundred years, two hundred, five hundred years seem a long, long time. Such time, however, is but a day to God!

Many scholars who read the Scriptures correctly in the view of current events, feel that we are living now in the latter days of life on this earth and that we have entered upon the final era—the last act of the mighty drama that started all those thousands of years ago in the Garden of Eden!

There are stirrings in the Middle East. Ancient Persia is once again a key nation because of oil. With the re-establishment of Israel as a separate nation, a sovereign state with its own currency, its own army, its own identity, the wheel has made its mighty cycle and is coming to a full turn. It was in that rich and fertile crescent of the Near East that our civilization had its beginning. From this restricted area it spread out in all directions. It encircled the globe. It moved steadily around, pausing sometimes to collect itself and gather strength, trapped sometimes in the mighty talons of man's many dark ages of barbarism, ignorance, godlessness, and fear. Until now at last, and in our time, it is beginning to return to the scene of its beginning.

In addition, these scholars look about them and see all too clearly the picture that Jesus painted when He said: "But as the days of Noah were, so shall also the coming of the Son of Man be. For as in the days that were before the flood they were eating and drinking, marrying and giving in marriage, until that day that Noah entered the ark. And knew not until the flood came and took them all away; so shall also the coming of the Son of Man be. Then shall two be in the field; the one shall be taken, and the other left. Two women shall be grinding at the mill; the one shall be taken and the other left. Watch therefore: for ye know not what hour your Lord doth come." [4]

These scholars point out (Daniel 12:4) where Daniel refers to the great increase in knowledge of the last days as another of the trends that indicates the approaching end. "Many shall run to and fro," this passage tells us, and we need no prompting to recognize the tremendous increase in both travel and knowledge that has marked these past fifty years. Never before in all recorded history have events been so speeded up, never before has one man-made wonder followed so closely the heels of others.

Medical men and psychiatrists for the past twenty-five years have been saying that the human body is not geared for such tension, that it cannot withstand so much speed and pressure, but we dash forward just the same. Many of the mighty leaders, whose work has made this drastic speed-up possible, have dropped dead at their desks, victims of the very Frankenstein monster they created!

We are told that Ezekiel 38 and 39 *may* well be describing Russia and the mighty power of Communism, in the great armies that shall rise and march against the Lord in the latter days.

Many intellectuals scoffed at 2 Peter 3:10-12 a few years ago, but the explosion of the hydrogen bomb and the terrible possibilities of the cobalt bomb have changed their skepticism to wonderment at the Bible predictions.

"But the day of the Lord will come as a thief in the night; in the which the heavens shall pass away with a great noise, and the elements shall melt with fervent heat, the earth also and the works that are therein shall be burned up. Seeing then that all these things shall be dissolved, what manner of persons ought ye to be in all holy conversation and godliness. Looking for and hasting unto the coming of the day of God, wherein the heavens being on fire shall be dissolved, and the elements shall melt with fervent heat?"

I would certainly not make the mistake of William Mil-

[4] *Matthew 24:37-42.*

ler, or of so many other sincere but overzealous men of
God, in setting even an approximate date for the return
of Christ. I do, however, in all seriousness point out that
the times in which we are living differ radically from any
that have gone before. The tempo is increased, events of
such magnitude that any one of them would have been
the sensation of the age a short time ago, now come so
close together that many pass almost unnoticed. Moral
laxness has become so common and so widely accepted
that little or no effort is made to conceal it. Corruption
in high places is almost taken as the rule rather than the
exception!

Above all we are faced with the mighty force of Communism—the greatest, most well-organized and outspoken
foe of Christianity that the church has confronted since
the days of pagan Rome! The anti-Christ, that the prophets warned would appear in the latter days, may be grow-
ing and taking concrete shape before our very eyes—A
bold, brazen, well-armed anti-Christ, who does not stoop
to disguise his identity or masquerade his purpose.

These are apocalyptic trends, marked by the war,
famine, pestilence and death that we know so well are
riding around the world at this very moment. Time, as
measured by heavenly bodies, may give us ten years, a
hundred years, a thousand years; but it may also give us
only a day, a week, a month. It may well be true now
"that this generation shall not pass, till all these things be
fulfilled." [5]

Until that *Day of Days* the attitude of every Christian
should be one of watching and expecting. Jesus said,
"Watch therefore, for ye know not what hour your Lord
doth come." [6] Again this thrilling hope should cause a
complete consecration to service on the part of all that
believe it. Jesus said, "Occupy till I come." [7] It is also to
be a time of preparation. Jesus said, "Be ye therefore
ready also, for the Son of Man cometh at an hour when
ye think not." [8]

[5] *Matthew 24:34.*   [6] *Matthew 24:42.*
[7] *Luke 19:13.*   [8] *Luke 12:40.*

All of history is moving toward that climactic day when all enemies shall have been put under His feet and Christ shall have been crowned. The Bible says, "Of the increase of His government and peace there shall be no end, upon the throne of David, and upon His kingdom, to order it, and to establish it with judgment and with justice from henceforth even for ever." [9]

In that day war and strife shall cease. Sin and want shall be no more. In that day sorrow and pain will be unknown. In that day the heathen will be converted. In that day no man shall dwell in ignorance of God. In that day all of nature shall unfold the splendor and luster that characterized Eden. In that day the very beasts of the earth will dwell together in amity and peace. In that day the knowledge of the love of God shall cover the earth. In that day our long and ardent prayer, "Thy kingdom come," shall be answered at last.

> *Jesus shall reign whe'er the sun*
> *Doth his successive journies run;*
> *His kingdom stretch from shore to shore,*
> *'Til moons shall wax and wane no more.*

This is *the* hope of the Christian!

[9] *Isaiah* 9:7.

Chapter Eighteen

PEACE—AT LAST

Thou wilt keep him in perfect peace, whose mind is stayed on Thee: because he trusted in Thee.

ISAIAH 26:3.

YOU know now what it means to be at peace with God. You know what it means to be a Christian. You know the price that has to be paid to get this illusive thing called peace and happiness. I know men who would write a check for a million dollars if they could find peace. Millions are searching for it. Every time they get close to finding the peace that you have found in Christ, Satan steers them away. He blinds them. He throws up a smoke screen. He bluffs them. And they miss it! But you have found it! It is yours now forever. You have found the secret of life.

There are many things you still do not understand. There are many mysteries. There are many problems that baffle you. But down underneath it all is that inward relaxation and peace that will lead to confident living. You have found that there are many advantages to the Christian ideal that challenge any other philosophical concept. Materialism, Communism, and all the other philosophical interpretations do not hold a candle to what Christ offers.

Dr. Thiessen in his work on *Christian Ethics* has listed several advantages which we will give here: First, there is *sonship*. The moment you accepted Jesus Christ as personal Savior you were adopted into the family of God. You are now His child. You have certain privileges and responsibilities that only royalty can know. Royal blood is in your veins by adoption. You have become a member of the family of the King of Kings and Lord of Lords.

Second, you are an *heir*. The Bible teaches that when you were born again, your new position in Christ has made you a joint heir with Christ. You are now heir to all things.

Third, there is *peace*. Peace can be experienced only when you have received divine pardon—when you have been reconciled to God and when you have harmony within, with your fellow man and especially with God. "There is no peace, saith my God, to the wicked." [1] But through the blood of the cross, Christ has made peace with God for us and is Himself our peace. If by faith we accept Him, we are justified by God and can realize the inner serenity that can come to man through no other means. When Christ enters our heart, we are freed of that haunting sense of sin. Cleansed of all feeling of contamination and unfitness, we can lift up our heads secure in the knowledge that we can look with confidence into the face of our fellow men. "When a man's ways please the Lord he maketh even his enemies to be at peace with him." Even more important, we know that we can stand before God in the hour of our death with this same feeling of peace and security. Communism nor any other philosophy can promise as much.

The fourth great benefit that is derived from a knowledge of Christ is *spiritual life*. In his natural state, no man is fully aware of the wrongness of his past life, but he is aware of the deadness of his soul. Those not acquainted with theological terms may not express their inner feelings in quite this way, but they are conscious of them. All natural men wonder at times at their own indifference to right and wrong. They are disturbed at their own willingness to compromise in the face of obvious injustices, to settle for the expedient thing rather than the right thing. Even the most calloused sinner experiences mo-

---

[1] *Isaiah 57:21.*

ments when he wishes he could be good. The most hard-
ened criminals, the most brazen prostitutes are all aware
of the deep, all-but-smothered longings within themselves
to be something better than they are. Unconverted men
and women who try to live a decent life are acutely aware
of how far short they fall of their goal, and the tragedy
is that so many of them do not even know that they are
failing because they are dead in sins and trespasses and
must be made alive through Christ before they can live
according to spiritual laws.

Jesus said, "I am come that they might have life, and
that they might have it more abundantly." [2] And Paul
stated, "If any man be in Christ, he is a new creature:
old things are passed away; behold, all things are become
new." [3]

To be born anew in Christ means to be born to new
ideals, new aspirations, new hopes, and new abilities to
achieve these fresh new goals. Christ as Lord and Master
has given you a new life. You have been born again.

Fifth, there is the *joy of Christian fellowship* that
comes from being a Christian. Loneliness is one of the
great terrors, the great tragedies of mankind. How often
we speak of feeling alone in the midst of a great crowd.
How many men and women have experienced a greater
sense of loneliness in a huge city than they have when
walking down a country road all by themselves. How
often we long to find someone who can understand and
share our innermost feelings, someone to whom we can
talk, who sees life as we see it, who is guided by the
same motives, who judges by the same values.

When in the popular phraseology of the day we talk
about finding someone who speaks our language, we are
really repeating the same longing that the Psalmist expressed when he said, "I looked on my right hand, and
beheld, but there was no man that would know me;
refuge failed me; no man cared for my soul." [4]

---

[2] *John 10:10.*   [3] *2 Corinthians 5:17.*
[4] *Psalm 142:4.*

You have found Christ to be the one Friend who understands your every thought, and once fellowship has been established with Him you can never be alone again. When Christ takes the rightful place in your heart, all sense of separation from God disappears. Once more you stand in the presence of God. This fellowship is a joy unspeakable and full of glory. No man-made philosophy can bestow this glorious benefit.

Sixth, there comes a *new strength* in following Christ. Man by himself is unable to attain his own standards, let alone attain the far higher and more exacting standards of God. The Mosaic laws were laid down as the minimum of behavior acceptable to God, and you are in yourself too weak to maintain even this standard unaided. Throughout history man has made resolution after resolution, hoping he would have the strength to keep them, but knowing in his heart that the best he could achieve would be a temporary reform and not a permanent change. This human weakness is so widely recognized that New Year's resolutions have become a worldwide joke and man's ability to turn over a new leaf without the help of God is subject to open scorn. It is only through rebirth in Christ that man can achieve, not just an alteration in his present way of life, but the creation of a new personality.

We are all familiar with the transformation that took place in Saul on the road to Damascus, when Christ entered his heart and changed him from one of His most destructive enemies to one of His mightiest advocates. Many equally dramatic changes in human personalities are taking place today, and they are being brought about by the selfsame means that transformed Saul into Paul— birth again through Jesus Christ!

There is no human philosophy that can achieve such changes or provide such strength. This mighty strength stands ready to be available at your beck and call at all times. God said, "Fear thou not; for I am with thee: be not dismayed; for I am thy God. I will strengthen thee;

yea, I will help thee; yea, I will uphold thee with the right hand of My righteousness." [5]

Whatever the circumstances, whatever the call, whatever the duty, whatever the price, whatever the sacrifice —His strength will be your strength in your hour of need.

Seventh, there are *physical benefits* that accrue from Christian living. Sin and the sense of inner unworthiness impair physical and mental well-being. The sense of physical impurity and physical immorality, the sense of hatred directed toward our fellow men, the awareness of our own inadequacy and frustration and our inability to achieve the goals to which we aspire—these are the real reasons for physical and mental illness. The sense of guilt and sin that natural man carries within himself renders him unfit for the performance of his duties, renders him sick in both mind and body. It was no accident that Jesus combined healing with His preaching and teaching when He was on earth. There is a very real relationship between the life of the spirit and the health of the body and mind.

Peace with God and the peace of God in a man's heart and the joy of fellowship with Christ have in themselves a beneficial effect upon the body and mind and will lead to the development and preservation of physical and mental power. Thus, Christ promotes the best interest of the body and mind as well as of the spirit, in addition to inward peace, the development of spiritual life, the joy and fellowship with Christ and the new strength that comes with being born again.

There are certain special privileges that only the true Christian can enjoy. There is, for example, the privilege of *having divine wisdom and guidance continually*. The Bible says, "If any of you lack wisdom, let him ask of God, that giveth to all men liberally, and upbraideth not; and it shall be given him." [6]

Also the Christian has a sense of *true optimism*, the assurance that according to divine revelation everything will turn out well in the end.

[5] *Isaiah 41:10.*   [6] *James 1:5.*

The Christian also has a *world view*. This world view sets forth God's purpose and the end toward which all are proceeding. It assures us that in spite of men's war upon each other and in spite of the destructive forces of nature which seem to hold us in their grip, God is still on the throne and in command of everything. Satan himself is held back by God's power and given an opportunity to exercise his evil influence only as God sees fit and only as long as God sees fit to let him do it. The Scriptures teach us that God has a definite plan for each period of history, for every nation and for every individual. The Scripture discloses God's plan for the return of Christ when His kingdom shall be established, as we have already seen. Thus, for the Christian, life has a plan and an assurance that God will ultimately triumph over all unrighteousness.

In summing up the superiority of the Christian life over all other ways of living we cannot overlook the advantage that the Christian will have for all eternity. Job said, "If a man die, shall he live again?" [7] He answered his own question when he said, "For I know that my Redeemer liveth and that He will stand at the latter day upon the earth." [8]

What a prospect! What a future! What a hope! What a life! I would not change places with the wealthiest and most influential man in the world. I would rather be a child of the King, a joint-heir with Christ, a member of the Royal Family of heaven!

I know where I've come from, I know why I'm here, I know where I'm going—and I have peace in my heart. His peace floods my heart and overwhelms my soul!

The storm was raging. The sea was beating against the rocks in huge, dashing waves. The lightning was flashing, the thunder was roaring, the wind was blowing; but the little bird was asleep in the crevice of the rock, its head serenely under its wing, sound asleep. That is peace: to be able to sleep in the storm!

[7] Job 14:14.   [8] Job 19:25.

In Christ we are relaxed and at peace in the midst of the confusions, bewilderments, and perplexities of this life. The storm rages, but our hearts are at rest. We have found peace—at last!